CHRISTIANITY 101 - 7 BIBLE BASICS AND BONUS BOOK: PURE CHRISTIANITY - THE ESSENCE OF BIBLICAL DISCIPLESHIP

BY BRIAN JOHNSTON

Copyright Hayes Press 2016

All rights reserved. No part of this book may be reproduced, stored in a retrieval system, or transmitted in any form, without the written permission of Hayes Press.

Published by:

HAYES PRESS Publisher, Resources & Media,

The Barn, Flaxlands

Royal Wootton Bassett

Swindon, SN4 8DY

United Kingdom

www.hayespress.org

Unless otherwise indicated, all Scripture quotations are from the HOLY BIBLE, the New King James Version® (NKJV®). Copyright © 1982 Thomas Nelson, Inc. Used by permission. All rights reserved." Scriptures marked NIV are from New International Version®, NIV® Copyright © 1973, 1978, 1984, 2011 by Biblica, Inc.™ Used by permission. All rights reserved worldwide. Scriptures marked NASB are from the New American Standard Bible®, Copyright © 1960, 1962, 1963, 1968, 1971, 1972, 1973, 1975, 1977, 1995 by The Lockman Foundation. Used by permission." (www.Lockman.org)

If you enjoyed reading this book and/or others in the series, we would really appreciate it if you could just take a couple of minutes to leave a brief review where you downloaded this book.

As a thank-you for downloading this book, please help yourself to a free download of "Healthy Churches – God's Bible Blueprint For Growth" by Brian Johnston in the Search For Truth Series:

Amazon.com: http://amzn.to/1FuoN5l

Amazon.co.uk: http://amzn.to/1HTSize

TABLE OF CONTENTS

BASIC BIBLE TRUTHS

CHAPTER ONE: WHAT'S THIS ABOUT BEING BORN AGAIN?

CHAPTER TWO: SALVATION IN THREE DIMENSIONS

CHAPTER THREE: EXPLAINING ETERNAL SECURITY

CHAPTER FOUR: THE A-B-C OF BIBLE READING

CHAPTER FIVE: POINTERS ON PRAYER

CHAPTER SIX: WONDERING ABOUT WATER BAPTISM?

CHAPTER SEVEN: DISCOVERING THE BIBLE'S PATTERN FOR SERVICE

PURE CHRISTIANITY: THE ESSENCE OF BIBLICAL DISCIPLESHIP

CHAPTER ONE: KNOWING CHRIST

CHAPTER TWO: ENJOYING CHRISTIAN FELLOWSHIP

CHAPTER THREE: BEING CHRISTLIKE

CHAPTER FOUR: WALKING THE WAY OF LOVE

CHAPTER FIVE: ABIDING IN THE TRUE VINE

FURTHER TITLES IN THIS SERIES

SEARCH FOR TRUTH RADIO BROADCASTS

CONTACTING SEARCH FOR TRUTH

CHAPTER ONE: WHAT'S THIS ABOUT BEING BORN AGAIN?

I remember in January 2004 while I was in the Philippines, reading in the Philippine Daily Inquirer newspaper about a moratorium on drug dealers. As a result of an appeal by the Pope their death sentence was postponed. The newspaper described those on death row waiting for their fate to be determined as being "the living dead of the Philippines". Some newspaper headlines are effective. That must have been one because I've never forgotten it.

But here's the point: as sinners in God's sight, everyone born - not only in the Philippines but anywhere in the world – is born with an eternal death sentence hanging over their head; in other words, we're all the living dead of this planet! We perhaps should explain further what being dead in this sense means. As judged by Jesus' illustration of the prodigal son (in Luke 15:24), it means to be disinterested in loving God or even communicating with God, who is represented by the father in Jesus' story. Again, it's just like how a light bulb disconnected from the electrical supply could be said to be "dead". So, "dead in sins" is how the Bible in Ephesians chapter 2 begins to describe those who don't know God.

And "the wages of sin is death", the Bible explains (Romans 6:23), which means that God's judgement on our sins will sentence us to remain for ever in this state of separation from him. Now, I'm not about to tell you about how that sentence can be postponed, or even about some indefinite moratorium, but to tell you about how God has actually made possible a way back to life for us – a way back to experiencing life in its fullest sense for ever.

But first, let's fully register the point that our own good works can't save us. This is because, as we've seen, we're actually dead in God's sight – because of our sins. That's why we can't even begin to hope that God will be pleased enough by our good works that he'll agree to let us into heaven. Please allow me to illustrate the thinking of many people, so that we can realize for ourselves just how utterly hopeless this kind of thinking is. Let's imagine a dispute between neighbours which comes before a local magistrate. One man is accused of stealing his neighbour's motorbike. Imagine he says this to the magistrate: 'I am here today to demand justice. I don't want mercy or compassion, I simply want my right to justice. In connection with the theft of the motorbike which I'm being accused of, I admit that I did it. But there have been many other days when I did not steal his motorbike. I have even done some good things for him on a few occasions. So, on that basis, I demand justice. I demand to be declared innocent and free to go!'

Now, let me ask you, what do you think the magistrate will say? Will he be convinced by this argument? No, of course not! And neither will God be convinced if we plead that our good works should cancel out our sins. We have to admit that things aren't looking good for us. But I'm here to tell you positively, that there's a way back to life with God and Calvary's cross where Jesus, God's Son, died for you, is the place where you begin.

But what does God require from us? How does Jesus' death on the cross for us actually become effective for each of us personally? Jesus said that unless someone is born again, he or she cannot experience the kingdom of God (John 3:3). What is this rebirth? One famous preacher once illustrated it something like this: suppose that in the U.K. there should be a law passed, that admission to a certain position in society could only be open to persons who were born in the U.K. This will allow us to illustrate the difference between behavioural changes that people make in themselves and the real, divine work of being born again. Suppose, then, that someone – say a 'First Nations' North American, for instance - should come to the U.K. to try to obtain this position – remember, the one for which the rule is that a person must be born in the U.K. in order to obtain the privilege. Suppose he says, "okay but I'll change my name, for an English name.' But that fails to impress the authorities for it's clear that he's not born and bred in the U.K.

"But," says our First Nations American friend, "I'm even prepared to renounce my native clothing, and adopt the latest U.K. fashions." But even this further attempt to qualify for the privilege he's seeking fails because the law, as we said, requires that he must be born in the country; and without that, whatever his clothing or fashion sense, he simply cannot get the position he's trying for. Let's just interrupt our illustration at this point to say that there are many who consider themselves to be Christian in name, and what's more, have also 'dressed themselves up' in the best of adopted Christian manners – perhaps even attending church regularly – but they're still not eligible for heaven.

"Well," says the First Nations American, "I'll not only adopt the U.K. dress fashion, but I'll learn their language too." He does that, and says, "Now that I've become thoroughly Anglicized; may I not be accepted?" However, of course, the answer is still 'No', and for the same reason: because his is not the correct birth. And so the additional point is that some people even talk like Christians, except that they're without a genuine Christian heart.

In summary, to have the name of a professing Christian, to have the appropriate manners or way of life, even to talk the language of the prayer-book or the hymn-book is not enough. Heaven is for those with the correct birth. To be a true Christian you must be born one – or should I say, reborn as one. Heaven is for those who have this second and spiritual birth.

We've just said that this new birth is spiritual, and so to begin to understand more about it, let's compare and contrast it with our natural birth. The natural birth of a baby is usually a source of joy for the parents, their family and friends. It's the beginning of a new life. Someone's born who's at the beginning of a life, with all the expectations that brings. But the new birth is a far bigger event than natural birth, for it's the beginning of eternal life - a life that'll never come to an end. When a baby is born, its name is registered in the population registers on earth, but when we're born again, our names are written in a book in heaven (Luke 10:20). The new birth brings so much joy with it, both in heaven and in earth. The angels in heaven rejoice over anyone who repents (Luke 15:10); and those on earth who already love God, also rejoice when someone is born again.

But is there really such a birth? The Bible says so. In fact, Jesus Christ himself, we may say, coined the expression. He was talking one evening to a high churchman of his day, someone called Nicodemus. Nicodemus was a fine upstanding pillar of society, a very religious man, but Jesus told him very plainly that he needed to be born again. Jesus went on to query Nicodemus' lack of understanding of this fact (John 3:10). It would seem Jesus expected him to have understood the words of one of the major Old Testament prophets as indicating such a new birth (Ezekiel 36:25,26). This new birth experience takes place by the work of God's Spirit (John 3:5,6) in anyone who believes in what God's Word says (1 Peter 1:23). Yes, it's a work the Spirit of God does in us through the Word of God. As the disciple Peter wrote, we've been born again "through the living and enduring word of God."

Which means it doesn't happen when we're baptized in water. No, water baptism can't bring about this kind of change. But it happens when we believe in the Bible, and what it says about Christ – and about us.

So, how can we be born again? Well, we must believe God's Word - everything in it with regard to ourselves and Christ. God tells us that "There is no-one righteous, not even one" (Romans 3:10). We've sinned against God who created us. We're alienated from him; by nature we don't love him. There's no part of our being that can possibly commend us to God – for ours is a futile mind; a darkened understanding; a calloused heart; and an impure sensuality with greed (see Ephesians 4:17-19). Do you see how sin has affected every part of our being? That's how the Bible describes us and we need to come to terms with it, with the unreserved realization that we're "dead" through our "trespasses and sins" (Ephesians 2:1), as we said before. That was the Bible text we began with, and that's why we must be born again. A behavioural change alone won't cut it, can't change our hearts - we need a new nature, and so a supernatural new birth. In short, we need a miracle in order to become acceptable to God!

The first step in this miraculous experience is to confess our sins to God, affirming that what he says about us is true. What does he say? He says we're sinners. The second step is: to believe in our hearts that Jesus Christ, God's Son, took our place and died for our sins. We have to say from the depths of our hearts: HE DIED FOR ME! We must turn to Jesus Christ, the only Saviour. This is our part in God's plan of salvation. God's part is to bring about the major change itself - the new birth - through God's Spirit coming to live within us. The Bible says, "But as many as received Him, to them He gave the right to become children of God, even to those who believe in his name; who were born not of blood, nor of the will of the flesh nor of the will of man, but of God" (John 1:12,13).

Can we know that we've been born again? We can for sure! We can know it with certainty because "The Spirit Himself bears witness with our spirit that we are children of God" (Romans 8:16). The Lord Jesus says, "Whoever hears my word and believes him who sent me, has everlasting life, and shall not come into judgment, but has passed from death into life" (John 5:24). Did you notice the ring of assurance in that text?

This eternal life - the born-again experience – means you're freed by the God who loves you, and you're accepted by the Saviour who died for you. Accept this offer - please don't fail to do so or you'll be forever lost. The life you have now, which started out in natural birth, is short and perhaps soon to end. Be wise, repent and accept Christ today.

Are you born again? Rejoice in God. Don't go back to the old way of life and live for yourself only. Give your life to him who died for you. Invite him every day to fellowship with you (Revelation 3:20). And he'll come – that's the amazing thing. Through his Spirit, he'll change your life, so you'll be able to say: "Christ lives in me." Make him known to others around you, because if you do, he'll confess you to the angels of God (Luke 12:8). Be a witnessing and joyful Christian. Feed the new life you now have through prayer, faith, and biblical Christian fellowship. Read daily in God's Word, for it's to our inner being what food is to our stomach. And may the Lord be with you in a powerful way as you enjoy the new life he freely gives.

CHAPTER TWO: SALVATION IN THREE DIMENSIONS

The Christian is someone who's been rescued and who, as a result of the spiritual deliverance which he or she has known, will always remain 'saved.' As we wish to go on to explain, this salvation of which the Bible speaks is a threefold or triple deliverance best described as having past, present and future aspects which we'll be labelling as "salvation from the penalty of sin"; "salvation from the power of sin"; and "salvation from the presence of sin". So that we might better understand these expressions, we'll deal with them in turn.

First then, let's tackle "salvation from the penalty of sin". "I am saved and I know it," cried a young man in the joy that flooded his heart after he'd accepted Christ as his Saviour. The assurance he knew then answered to the words of First John, "that you may know that you have eternal life" (1 John 5:13). It's for all who share in this "common salvation" (Jude 3) which is by grace through faith (Ephesians 2:8), that we're discussing this.

On the cross, Jesus "bore our sins in his body on the tree" (1 Peter 2:24). In total solitude, even forsaken by his God, he suffered in our place, to save us from the judgment which the Bible plainly tells us that our sins deserve (Romans 6:23). He did this for us, as our willing substitute, so that "he might bring us safely home to God" (1 Peter 3:18 NLT). Paul puts it so succinctly: "Christ died for our sins" (1 Corinthians 15:3). He's done everything for our salvation and now God only asks of us that we repent and believe in him in order for us to be saved. Let's be quite clear - it's not a reward for services rendered. Far from it, this is God's gift of grace to all who believe. It's not something which is of ourselves as "salvation is of the Lord" (Jonah 2:9) nor is it something that we ourselves have earned by our own good works (see Ephesians 2:9). As a result, we've absolutely nothing to boast about.

I once read about an instant cake mix that was a big flop. The instructions said all you had to do was add water and bake. The company couldn't understand why it didn't sell - until their research discovered that the buying public felt uneasy about a mix that required only water. Apparently people thought it was too easy. They made additional contributions – and failed to make successful cakes. Likewise, all the honour and glory for our salvation from the penalty which our sins truly deserve before a holy God is God's and his alone. There is nothing we have to, nor can, add to Christ's finished work. God's recipe for us to be saved from the penalty of our sins is faith alone.

I'm reminded of a note I received from a young man in another country. He was describing a man he'd been witnessing to. He referred to him as an 'SSBG'. He intended each letter to stand for a word which begins with that letter. I wonder then what an SSBG refers to? There's a clue in the great Bible verse we've already referred to - Ephesians 2:8: "For by grace you have been saved through faith; and that not of yourselves, it is the gift of God."

Yes, he was telling me about a **S**inner **S**aved **B**y **G**race! I can tell you straight away that I'm one of those too – as I hope you are also. Because, you know, we're all sinners as Romans 3 verse 23 says; there are only two kinds of people in the world: saved sinners and sinners who don't have a saviour.

But before I forget, let me tell you more about the man my young friend was describing to me in this way. To avenge the death of his son by communist rebels in 1987, this man – who lived in the Philippines - committed multiple rape and murder which resulted in him receiving a 20-year prison sentence. But in prison he repented of the evils he'd done, received Christ and began to study his Bible. In due course, he was released from prison, having served his sentence. My young friend now takes up the report: "when we arrived at his home testifying of God's grace, he also was not ashamed to testify to his neighbours."

Sarenas truly was a sinner saved by grace. Perhaps you regard him as having done such terrible crimes that he doesn't deserve to know personal forgiveness from God? Maybe right now you're comparing your own life with his, and it could very easily be that it's much more respectable. But salvation is not something which any one of us deserves – neither Sarenas, nor you, nor I. Let's repeat our Bible text in Ephesians 2:8: "For by grace you have been saved through faith; and that not of yourselves, it is the gift of God." And that same verse goes on to say that salvation is not of works so that no one can boast. The word "grace" means God's undeserved favour which he shows to us in granting any one of us salvation, in other words the forgiveness of our sins.

During the Spanish-American War, Theodore Roosevelt came to Clara Barton of the Red Cross to buy some supplies for his sick and wounded men. His request was refused. Roosevelt was troubled and asked, "How can I get these things? I must have proper food for my sick men." "Just ask for them, Colonel", said Barton. "Oh", said Roosevelt, "then I do ask for them." He got them at once through grace, not through purchase. (Illustration for Biblical Preaching by Michael P. Green p.176).

Have you turned to God (and away from your sins) and humbly asked him – only asked him - and asked without offering payment in kind – to save you and grant you pardon for the sinner you are and the sins which you've done?

Let's now turn our attention to the second dimension, which is "salvation from the power of sin". The person who's done what we've just described is already a new creation (2 Corinthians 5:17), reborn with a nature that's from God (John 3:3-5). However, the old nature is still present, so that once we're saved, we begin to feel the battle between the flesh and the Spirit (Galatians 5:17). The Apostle Paul shared his experience like this: "I am not practicing what I would like to do, but I am doing the very thing I hate" (Romans 7:15). But - and for this we give thanks to God - the Bible provides the solution to this problem which I'm sure we can all identify with, if we're honest. God doesn't save us and then leave us to our fate. Not at all, he's sent his Holy Spirit to live in our hearts that we might be given power over sin, and power to live a holy and victorious life for Jesus. We have the indwelling Spirit of God by whom to strive to overcome indwelling sin. We're urged to consider ourselves "to be dead to sin, but alive to God in Christ Jesus" (Romans 6:11). In Romans 8 we're told how the Holy Spirit works in us to give us victory, so that we may know a triumphant life.

The following are four suggestions to help us to live for Christ:

1. We must hate sin. Consider sin as it is in reality - disobedience to God. When we do wrong, let's immediately confess it to God and claim the promise of cleansing (1 John 1:9).

2. Let's take time each day for quiet reflection on God's Word, asking the Lord to speak to us through what we've read (James 1:21).

3. We should try to maintain an unhurried time of prayer every day, preferably in the morning. This is how, by God's help, which we ask for, we renew our strength. No-one can be strong without this (Isaiah 40:3).

4. We need to allow the Holy Spirit to control our lives. "If we live by the Spirit, let us also walk by the Spirit" (Galatians 5:25). Since the Spirit is the source of our life, we should also let him determine its course, by our obedience to God's Word.

If we give serious attention to these things, we can expect salvation from the power of sin for it is God who works in us for his glory (Philippians 2:12-13).

And finally, we come to consider salvation from the presence of sin. What a joyful day it will be when we're called to heaven to be with the Lord Jesus Christ! From then on, sin will trouble us no more. Our sinful nature will be a thing of the past, and our new bodies will be changed to be like Jesus' own glorified body. This will happen when the Lord Jesus comes back, and the dead in Christ shall rise again and those who are still alive and believe in him will be changed and snatched up with them from the earth. Together we will meet the Lord in the clouds (1 Thessalonians 4:13-18).

Every day brings this glorious expectation nearer: "for now salvation is nearer to us than when we believed" (Romans 13:11). God intends that we should live in daily expectation of the Lord's return. This hope will keep our minds on the things that are above, where Christ is seated at God's right hand (Colossians 3:1,2). When this day comes our salvation will be complete in all three of its aspects which we've been studying. We'll then obtain the outcome of our faith which is the salvation of our souls (1 Peter 1:9).

It should hopefully now go without saying that this final aspect of salvation is as certain as the first aspect is secure. The present dimension of our salvation (which is the second as we've listed them), namely that of experiencing deliverance from the power of sin in our lives day by day, is the only aspect of our salvation which actually does depend on us co-operating with the promptings of the Holy Spirit. This must be kept firmly in its biblical perspective to prevent us from being troubled by any misrepresentation of the danger of "falling away" (see Hebrews 6:6, where it relates to falling away from the confident hope of the Christian disciple in serving his or her Lord together with other disciples in the way the Lord has specified) – that has nothing to do with our past deliverance from sin's penalty.

It's only in the sense of overcoming sin's power from day to day that any of our works contribute in any way. They most emphatically don't count for anything in the matter of our escape from the judgement to come upon sinners without a saviour – which was settled once and for all in the past. Otherwise, this would plainly contradict the very plain and repeated assurance of Ephesians 2:8-9 (and such a contradiction cannot exist for God's Word cannot be broken - see John 10:35).

CHAPTER THREE: EXPLAINING ETERNAL SECURITY

God wants us to fully rejoice in his gift of eternal life, and his blessings of peace and joy (Romans 15:13). John wrote, "These things have I written unto you, that you may know that you have eternal life, you who believe in the name of the Son of God" (1 John 5:13).

Some, however, teach the false doctrine that the Christian believer can be saved and then lost again. This error is the result of confusing salvation with service. If you read 1 Corinthians 9:24-27 where the Apostle Paul talks about the possibility of being disqualified, you'll see that Paul's not talking about God's gift of salvation, but about serving the Lord by staying legitimately in contention for a prize – in the same way as an athlete needs to remain within the rules of the competition so as not to be barred from it. We can't compete to earn eternal life, because it's a gift. But after we've received the gift, Christians strive to serve well to earn the reward of an eternal crown. While we can be disqualified from that prize, this doesn't affect our eternal life.

Believers are children of God because they're born of God. Our heavenly Father may be disillusioned by our behaviour and our service, but we can never cease to be his children. We ask again, can disbelief, or an act of misconduct, or committing a crime, or any other thing rob anyone of the salvation that's found in Christ? It's not a new assertion to say that a backslider may lose his or her salvation, for the Apostle Paul evidently debated with those who claimed just that. They raised the objection to Paul's preaching which is implied by the opening words of Romans chapter 6:

"What shall we say then? Are we to continue in sin that grace may abound?" In other words, Paul must have been preaching "once saved, always saved", because of the fact that some were clearly reacting against it back then, effectively saying: "Come on, Paul, do you really mean to say that someone who's known salvation by placing personal faith in Christ can then live carelessly without any fear of losing his or her salvation?" 'If that's the case," they argued, "we might as well all sin at every opportunity if that means it gives God more opportunities to be gracious in forgiving our many sins!"

In that sixth chapter of Romans, Paul shows how wrong-headed this point of view is. He replies by saying in Romans 6:2: "By no means! How can we who died to sin still live in it?" This is the basis of Paul's rejection of their "we may as well live as we please" philosophy. He tells them that the reality is that the believer on the Lord Jesus Christ has in fact "died to sin." But what does this mean? Paul also tells us that "Christ died to sin." There must be a consistency between what it means for Christ to die to sin, and what it means for the believer to die to sin - since both these expressions are used in the same place in our Bible.

Paul reasons that, if Christ died to sin, and if we're identified with Christ, then it follows that we, too, died to sin – and as a practical consequence it would be out of place for us to now lead a life dominated by sinful practices. That's the sense of the flow of this paragraph in our Bibles. And to prove that we have indeed been identified with Christ, Paul shares two things: a revelation of what happened at our conversion, and an explanation of the meaning of our water baptism.

First, it's at salvation, when by God's grace we are saved through faith, that we were identified with the Christ of the cross in his death and resurrection. When we believe, it's as if Christ's death becomes our death and it's then that we receive new life in Christ.

Later, in water baptism we demonstrate that fact by "acting it out" – i.e., by being buried in water and rising again. Water baptism is only a symbolic witness to all who watch it about our previous identification with a crucified and resurrected Saviour.

There are so many other ways of assuring ourselves biblically of our eternal security in Christ, but the one that I personally find the most persuasive is the fact that the Bible teaches us that the primary salvation decision is God's not ours - which means that any view which permits us to lose our salvation seriously underplays God's sovereignty.

Jesus invited people to come to him and to rest in the knowledge of sins forgiven. In itself that famous invitation at the end of Matthew chapter 11 invites people to stop relying on their own efforts to obtain salvation, and simply come and rest in the salvation which Christ is offering as a gift. But in John chapter 6, the Lord pulls the curtain further back to reveal something of the bigger picture of what's involved in a sinner coming to Christ. He says: "All that the Father gives me will come to me, and whoever comes to me I will never cast out ... No one can come to me unless the Father who sent me draws him."

So, standing behind our coming to Christ in personal faith, is God's sovereign choice of each one of us who believes on the Lord Jesus. We find additional clarity on this point in the letter to the Ephesians, and its opening verses: "Blessed be the God and Father of our Lord Jesus Christ, who has blessed us in Christ with every spiritual blessing in the heavenly places, even as he chose us in him before the foundation of the world, that we should be holy and blameless before him" (Ephesians 3:1-4).

A moment's reflection ought to show us that if these things are so - if the matter of our salvation and eternal destiny has been of concern to God from before the foundation of the world - then it's highly unlikely that we should be able to toss it away on a whim, or even by a later quite deliberate rejection. Loss of faith in a believer is tragic, and brings about a loss of enjoyment of the assurance of salvation, but salvation itself as God's sovereign gift remains, having been underwritten by God's own choice from before this universe came into being. The outcome is already finalized in God's purpose (Ephesians 2:6; Romans 8:30) – as far as God is concerned it's as if we're already seated and glorified with Christ!

"You are severed from Christ, you who would be justified by the law; you have fallen away from grace." These strong words are found in Galatians 5:2-4. This was Paul's answer to those who had been saved through faith, prior to wondering if they should then bolster it with circumcision. This passage is decisive as to the fact that there can be no mixture of any kind between grace and works. Works don't come into the obtaining of salvation; nor are they regarded as necessary for holding on to salvation afterwards.

But sometimes these verses have been distorted in their meaning and made to suggest quite the opposite of Paul's argument: that we can be severed from Christ and fall away from grace in the loss of our actual salvation! That's not at all what Paul's saying here. Instead, he says, pure reliance on Christ on the one hand, and the desire to depend in some way on human effort on the other, belong in totally different categories - such that seeking to even maintain our salvation by some effort of our own transfers us from the one "camp" to the other. In that sense we're cut off from being able to proclaim "Christ alone". We've fallen away from the advocacy of "grace alone." By no longer operating in the sphere of "Christ alone" and "grace alone", we lose all certainty and enjoyment of the salvation God's provided for us in the one finished work of his own Son upon the cross (John 19:30).

Of course, this is what Paul consistently taught. You remember he taught the Philippian jailor "believe on the Lord Jesus Christ and you will be saved", but just suppose for a moment that the gift of salvation is subsequently conditional upon our own good works, then we can't possibly know if we've done well enough to still keep hold of it or not; so Paul's note of confident assurance to the jailor that "you will be saved" would then ring false.

At the future, personal assessment of our life of Christian service there will be the possibility of reward or loss of reward depending on our performance. Listen to how the apostle Paul puts it in First Corinthians chapter 3: "each man's work will become evident; for the day will show it because it is to be revealed with fire, and the fire itself will test the quality of each man's work. If any man's work which he has built on it remains, he will receive a reward. If any man's work is burned up, he will suffer loss; but he himself will be saved, yet so as through fire" (1 Corinthians 3:13-15).

Each Christian is a builder. In terms of the figure of speech Paul's using here, we either build with stuff that cannot burn or with stuff that can burn. The person building with stuff that burns is the backslider, who's not following God's plan or not doing the things God wants him or her to do – or who maybe is doing things that seem fine, but the motivation behind them is all wrong. At that future personal assessment of our Christian service which we'll each have with Christ, there'll be a fiery testing of our works – it'll be the flame test. If it burns, it wasn't any good.

Imagine the worst then that could happen for a Christian. They watch all their life's works go up in smoke. They lose, therefore, all their potential reward – there's nothing left for which to be rewarded. Nothing has withstood the fire. But what about the individual concerned? Did you catch Paul's reassuring words in this baseline case? "If any man's work is burned up, he will suffer loss; but he himself will be saved, yet so as through fire."

Ah, thank God for that! So then, here's what we are seeing from our Bibles: there are rewards for faithful service which we may fail to gain as distinct from the gift of salvation itself. Salvation itself is not a reward. It cannot be lost. But we may in some sense "suffer loss." That means the loss of potential rewards we may have gained if we'd lived a pleasing life to God's glory.

When a person professes faith in Christ (as the Apostle Peter famously did by declaring Jesus to be the Christ, the son of the living God) he or she also is built by Christ into his Church and is in fact baptized by Christ in the Holy Spirit into that Church which is known biblically as Christ's Body. This is the Lord's action, and in this case this is confirmed by the stated fact that the greatest known power could not overpower Christ's Church. We should check that again, it comes from the Lord's words in Matthew 16:18 – here they are once more: "I will build My church; and the gates of Hades will not overpower it."

Did you get that? After confirming his identity to Peter while at Caesarea Philippi, Christ proceeded to state the glorious purpose he was about – namely building his Church, comprised of all true believers of this age of grace (from the cross to the so-called Rapture event). Then he added that nothing, no power, not even the greatest power known to the ancient world, the power of death and the underworld, could defeat this great divine purpose. Psalm 16:10 prophesied that Christ's soul in death went down into Sheol or Hades, the realm of the dead. But the same disciple Peter says later in his preaching to the Jews in Acts chapter 2 (v.24) that Jesus couldn't possibly be held there in death, but God raised him up.

If God hadn't raised up Christ from the dead, if the gates of Hades had not been forced to yield for him, then this great church-building purpose of the ages would have been overpowered – but it wasn't, nor could it be! Praise God for that! Surely this fact of the gates of Hades and death not being able to overpower Christ's purpose in his Church also removes any possibility of the threat of dismemberment of a single believer from that Body, that Church. After all, who's going to mutilate or maim Christ's Body?! Our place in the Body of Christ is absolutely secured at conversion. Through the baptism in the Spirit which takes place automatically for each believer as they receive Christ (1 Corinthians 12:13), we're incorporated eternally into the Body of Christ which remains without any defect whatsoever (Ephesians 5:27).

In the same way that we might make use of recognized landmarks in giving someone directions, it's just as necessary to identify the Bible's main or landmark teachings and then navigate our way around individual and sometimes difficult verses in relation to them. If our understanding of a particular text seems to be at odds with one of the Bible's main teachings, it may indicate that the text should be related to a different teaching instead.

One such landmark teaching is that a truly born-again person through faith in Jesus is secure in God's keeping so far as his salvation from eternal judgement is concerned. Such a person is seen as 'in Christ', a status granted when he or she first believed. But there's another equally clear landmark teaching which is that as the believer travels daily nearer his assured heavenly home he or she is accountable to the Lord Jesus for their response to the will of God. These two landmark biblical teachings are distinct but complementary. One line gives the believer utmost assurance of salvation from his deserved eternal judgement in the lake of fire; but the other establishes that such grace in salvation mustn't be lightly regarded. We need to add on our part all diligence, in our faith supplying virtue, knowledge, self-control, patience, godliness and love of the brethren (2 Peter 1:5-8).

CHAPTER FOUR: THE A-B-C OF BIBLE READING

The Apostle Paul urged his protégé, Timothy, to pay attention to Bible reading – and if that was in public - then how much more in private also (see 1 Timothy 4:13). The kings of Israel were commanded by God to read God's Word daily (Deuteronomy 17:18,19). The Lord himself, in his humanity, by his frequent quotation of the Old Testament, displayed clear evidence of memorisation that surely came from a personal Scripture reading habit. All of which means we should follow their example.

Life's best advice is found in the Bible: "How blessed is the man who does not walk in the counsel of the wicked, nor stand in the path of sinners, nor sit in the seat of scoffers! **But his delight is in the law of the LORD, and in His law he meditates day and night.** He will be like a tree firmly planted by streams of water, which yields its fruit in its season and its leaf does not wither; and in whatever he does, he prospers" (Psalm 1:1-3).

Using the imagery of a riverside tree, Psalm 1 assures us that love for the Word of God will result in us being "firmly planted", yielding "fruit", without withering, but always prospering. In other words, it's saying that a passion for Bible-reading will tend to promote in our lives a sense of stability; that is, being settled in our convictions and spiritual lifestyle as well as being productive in our service and experiencing vitality and prosperity – those latter qualities, of course, being primarily in the spiritual sense.

We develop a passion for God through reading his Word – when God opens the Scriptures to us and opens our eyes, mind and heart to them. We read to enjoy him. Delighting in God's Law (Psalm 1), or Bible, is closely connected with delighting in the Lord himself (see Psalm 37). Just as we look through, not at, a microscope; we read the Bible to get to know God better.

It's reassuring when we confirm for ourselves that the Bible we have is true to the original form in which it was first communicated. It's well-established, and widely reported – so easy to check out – that from among all ancient literature nothing comes even remotely close to the Bible in passing the standard literary tests for a book being true to its original form. What's more, by making painstaking comparisons between thousands of early language fragments, experts, working like detectives, are able to make a strong case for knowing pretty well exactly what the original text of the Bible said – and based on that knowledge, we can be confident that our English language Bibles are reliable.

The Bible is such a special book from God. He's its ultimate author, and it's His revelation to us, which has been affirmed by lots of its predictions having been fulfilled with exact precision. So, it's no doubt very special, but in the main we're meant to read it like any other book, taking its words to have their normal meanings. And it's not written much like a textbook: for much of the time God instructs us through narrating the life experiences of others. We begin to gain a clear sense of what God approves in their lives which we can then begin to apply in our own life. There's no situation in life for which we can't find guidance - at least in principle – from this vast store of human encounters with God. As we read its pages regularly, we'll find our attention is often drawn to certain statements it makes and we begin to sense their particular relevance to decisions we have pending, as well as to other of life's experiences. So, the greatest wonder of the Bible is that God speaks to us through its pages.

Two of the earliest followers of Jesus said in Luke 24:32: "Were not our hearts burning within us while He was speaking to us on the road, while He was explaining the Scriptures to us?" We, too, can have the same experience whenever we sit down with a mature Christian friend or with a reputable study book, and after asking the Lord's help in prayer, we begin to enjoy a time of Bible study.

Long ago, using the parts of the Bible available to him then, the psalmist said: "I ... see wonderful things ... from Your Law" (Psalm 119:18). That reminds me of how, after 15 years of financing excavations in the Valley of the Kings with scarcely anything to show for his expenditure, Lord Carnarvon began to wonder if it would all prove fruitless. But then came an excited telegram from Howard Carter telling him to come to Luxor immediately. On 26 November 1922, Carter and Lord Carnarvon stood in front of the sealed door of Tutankhamun's tomb. Carter made a small hole in the door and then inserted a candle. Answering Carnarvon's anxious question, "Can you see anything?" Carter famously replied, "Yes, wonderful things." And there are wonderful things to be discovered in the pages of our Bible. Things which will warm our hearts, feed our souls, and draw us into close fellowship with the Lord. These blessings will be ours if we approach our reading prayerfully, asking for the eyes of our heart to be opened in the Spirit's working.

Let's not forget how valuable the Bible is – as is our daily reading of it. Dr Lehman Strauss talked about having "The Word of God" stamped on the spine of his rebound Bible – as an ever-present visible reminder that this was not just a book, but in reality "The Word of God." As such, it should have a unique place in all our lives. Thomas Aquinas is reputed to have used the Latin phrase "hominem unius libri timeo" (meaning "I fear the man of a single book"). But Aquinas' phrase was consciously turned on its head by John Wesley who said: "He came from heaven; He hath written it down in a book. O give me that Book! At any price, give me the Book of God. I have it; here is knowledge enough for me. Let me be homo unius libri!" (or the man of one Book).

John Wesley was certainly captivated by the Bible, so much so that one historian wrote of him: "... from the unlikely soil of a grossly immoral, drink-sodden nation of brutalized gamblers on the verge of collapse into absolute infidelity, [there] sprang under God and through Wesley the great awakening, the evangelical revival of the 18th century, which doubtless spared England a revolution such as befell the French" – such was the impact, under God, of only one man captivated by the Bible. May we also be captivated by its pages!

This is the formula for spiritual growth in the adventure of a Christian life recently begun: "like newborn babies, long for the pure milk of the word, so that by it you may grow in respect to salvation" (1 Peter 2:2). Read a little each day, read systematically, and occasionally study Bible characters and topics. Vary your diet with all parts of the Bible. Read, and grow in the grace and knowledge of the Lord you follow. And as we read, the promise is you and I will become more like him as 2 Corinthians 3:18 says: "we all, with unveiled face, beholding as in a mirror the glory of the Lord, are being transformed into the same image from glory to glory, just as from the Lord, the Spirit."

Finally, some practicalities. Let's try to answer in a little more detail four basic questions often asked in connection with the reading of the Bible.

1. Why should we read?

Well, for two reasons: (i) to gain knowledge - if you've accepted Jesus as Saviour, you'll want to know him better, love him more deeply and follow him more closely. This should be the life-goal of every Christian (Philippians 3:8-10) (ii) to grow – "... grow in the grace and knowledge of our Lord and Saviour Jesus Christ" (2 Peter 3:18). To become strong Christians, we need a daily intake of God's Word (1 Peter 2:2).

2. What should we read?

It's best to choose a version approved by other Christians, and suited to our reading level. And what about Bible helps? To help you to find a particular verse in the Bible, a concordance has an alphabetical arrangement of Biblical words; while commentaries provide explanations of the text. It's useful to use such books for study, but we should try to avoid reading more about the Bible than the Bible itself.

3. How should we read?

Reading a short passage, at least once a day, is vital. Make it short enough so that you can remember some words or verses throughout the day. There are several Bible reading plans available which allow you to read the whole Bible in say, one or three years. It's also a sensible practice to keep a fixed time reserved for a longer read. Some shorter books can be read in one sitting, the longer in several stages. Bible books have a dominant message and reading them in their entirety helps us to find it. On the way, we'll encounter memorable verses which will have their own impact upon us. Also, take time to 'dig deeper' into the meanings of Bible words and the implications of the stories of the Bible. It's also good to explore the major themes of the Bible.

There'll always be something that puts us under pressure at any hour of the day. But if we miss our daily time with the Bible, it'll be at the expense of our spiritual development. Try to make contact with God's Word in the morning. Perhaps the short read that was discussed earlier. Many get up early in the morning in order to read for a longer time and think it over, and they testify to the benefit of doing that. But in the evenings the Bible can also have a cleansing effect as we review the day. It may be that an entire evening or a large part of it, or even a weekend, can be occasionally devoted to the deeper study we mentioned. There's real profit from the self-discipline of reading the Bible.

But life can get so busy, and we'll need to each make a deliberate lifestyle choice. Just as Mary of Bethany did, as we read of her in Luke's Gospel chapter 10 and verse 39: "Mary ... was seated at the Lord's feet, listening to His word ..." The Lord affirmed her action, by saying: "Mary has chosen the good part" (Luke 10:39-42) and from that we can understand how we too can know the Lord's approval by taking time out with his Word.

A successful and enjoyable time of Bible-reading involves:

Prayer: this is a must; short - maybe; simple – yes; but always ask God's help when his book is opened. Then the Holy Spirit, as the Lord Jesus said: "shall take of mine, and shall show you" (John 16:15). The Holy Spirit inspired the texts that you're reading. He knows exactly what they mean and how they apply to your situation. Of course, seeking the Spirit's help is essentially done through prayer – where all effective Bible Study begins and ends.

Discipline: a resolute decision to read regularly and consistently (1 Timothy 4:13-15). Also commit to studying the Bible with other Bible students by belonging to a Biblical church of God, and, also by owning a set of approved commentaries on the whole Bible.

Meditation: Take time to reflect silently on what you read (Psalm 119:115). By "reflecting" we mean asking questions about the text and figuring out the answers from the context.

Respect: Treat God's living word with reverence (Ezra 9:4; Isaiah 66:2). The Bible itself is your greatest treasure under God. Try searching elsewhere in the Bible for words you find in a particular verse. Computer Bible programs are freely available. Find one that makes clicking on a word and searching its other uses in the same book or by the same author or in the whole New or Old Testament as easy as possible. It's amazing the help we can get when other sections of the Bible involving the same idea are considered.

CHAPTER FIVE: POINTERS ON PRAYER

In praying, it's helpful to begin by learning from a child's basic vocabulary: "sorry, thanks, please." For example, in the psalms of the Bible - which are prayers after all - the four key responses that come up again and again are: "Wow", "Sorry", "Thanks!" and "Help!". As we mature in spiritual things, it's good when a more experienced Christian can show us how to be thoughtful in prayer, as when the Apostle Paul prayed "With this in mind ..." (2 Thessalonians 1:11 NIV).

Prayer is one of the great privileges of a Christian - to have spiritual communion with the Almighty. Think of Abraham, Moses, Joshua, Hannah, David, Daniel, Esther, Nehemiah, Paul and many others and you'll see that men and women who had a strong faith and were used by God, were those who had a vibrant prayer life. Effective prayer is speaking with the Father, in the name of the Son, and by the Holy Spirit who is in us. Jesus said, "whatever you shall ask in my name, that will I do, that the Father may be glorified in the Son" (John 14:13).

Praying like that is the way God's chosen to bring his blessings to his children. It also emphasizes the personal relationship we have with God. More than that, in the act of praying we acknowledge that God is sovereign. That means we're to pray according to his will, and in line with his values. We're to pray with a clear conscience and a clean heart in conformity with God's character, and consistently with his revealed purposes. These are among the conditions for answered prayer and living in the joy of it. In that way, we claim in prayer those things which are his promises to us. But how do we go about it?

Where can we get to know God's will and what his values are? In the Bible, of course. The more we relate our prayer requests to what it reveals, the better. We must always rely on the Holy Spirit's guidance: not only praying in the Word, but praying in the Spirit. Prayer is so important for a Christian, that the Holy Spirit will help us when we don't even know how we should pray. The Spirit moves our hearts so that we're able to ask according to God's will (Romans 8:26). When our prayer is led by the Holy Spirit, it's effective. This is praying in the Holy Spirit (Jude 20).

Many Christians use the expression "having their Quiet Time" to mean the time they set aside each day for stilling their souls in the presence of God. When we prepare to enjoy fellowship with our Maker. It's good to shut ourselves off from a hundred and one everyday things that clutter our lives and minds. It's also wise to set a daily, regular time to pray, and the best is at the start of the day. Make this your quiet time. Let nothing hold you back from spending time with God. When we stick to this, it'll be a time of spiritual refreshment, in communion with God, praising him and pouring out our hearts to him (Psalm 5:2-4; 62:6-9).

There's no better advice than the Lord's when he counselled us to have a particular place to retire to where we can be free from interruptions, where we can disentangle ourselves from our daily duties; and from the worries and pressures that come with life. Two things which belong together are praying and watching (which includes ring-fencing our time commitment, as well as looking out for answers).

I don't know whether your habit is to pray out loud or whether you pray silently during your personal prayers at home. The Bible records the Lord's instruction as being: "When you pray *say*, Our Father in heaven ..." etc. It's often helpful to pray audibly even in private and to "say" the prayer rather than to just "think" it. It can be an aid to concentration when we actually put it into spoken words – it helps to guard against wandering thoughts or skating too glibly over a range of different issues without any real depth of thought. This habit is even a help when it comes to breaking "the sound barrier" of audibly praying with others.

Also, while we're on practical things, in personal prayer, it's good to kneel as did Daniel (Daniel 6:10). This shows our humility before God, for he's a great God and a great King (Psalm 95:3). It was the Lord Jesus himself who taught us in Matthew chapter 6: "When you pray, go into your room, and when you have shut your door, pray to your Father who is in the secret place; and your Father who sees in secret will reward you openly" (v.6 NKJV). Early African converts to Christianity were serious about praying. Each had a separate spot in the woods where he would pray. The paths to these became well worn. If someone began to neglect prayer, it was soon apparent to the others who advised: "Brother, the grass grows on your path."

But that doesn't always mean that praying comes naturally, as easy as breathing. The Bible itself recognizes there will be times when we don't know how to pray as we ought. And if you're like me from time to time you'll be jolted into realising just how shallow your prayer life has become. There may well be times, too, when we feel spiritually dry and not at all in the right frame of mind for praying. Of course, these are the times when we need prayer all the more. If we persevere with the discipline of prayer even when it feels more like a duty than genuine devotion, and speak to God about how we feel, we'll soon find the exercise once more becomes a delight.

The Lord had something to say about this: "He also spoke a parable unto them ... that men ought always to pray and not become discouraged" (Luke 18:1). In that section of Luke chapter 18, by means of two parables on the topic of prayer, the Lord Jesus taught the value, indeed the requirement, of persistent faithful praying and true humility. In other words, don't give up even when you're tempted to do so, and aim to have the right attitude and avoiding the pride that makes us critical or jealous of others.

As regards prayer there's no restriction, only in our faith. We must ask in accordance with God, knowing that he can do more than we actually are asking and thinking (Ephesians 3:20). The Lord promised, "Ask, and it shall be given; seek, and you shall find; knock, and it shall be opened" (Matthew 7:7).

No sin may remain hidden in our hearts, no anger or resentment toward others, if our praying is to be effective. This grieves the Holy Spirit and hinders us in prayer (Ephesians 4:30-32). If others have caused us harm, we should pray about it first, then talk about it with them and forgive them. If we've sinned in any way, we ought to confess this to God, and ask him for forgiveness in the name of the Lord Jesus (1 John 1:7-9). By the blood of Jesus we're cleansed from sin and forgiven and our prayers will then be answered. "The prayer of the upright is his delight" (Proverbs 15:8). He's delighted to answer such prayer.

As we grow in our faith and in our prayer life, there will be more and more things and people we can pray for. Some Christians have a prayer list, with the names of persons and different things noted, depending on the need. The more we pray for others, the more the Spirit of God uses us to help them. The more we pray for others, the stronger we will be ourselves. Our spiritual strength and vitality depends to a large extent on our prayer life. Someone once said, "No prayer - no power; little prayer - little power; much prayer – much power." The Apostle Paul often begins his Bible letters with an acknowledgement of God's grace in others, an expression of gratitude as well as joy, and a reference to his prayerfulness. These things reflect a passionate spirituality.

We must also remember that our heavenly Father already knows the things that we need even before we ask them him (Matthew 6:7-8). But he often waits until we tell him what our needs are, even though he already knows them. But we shouldn't come to him with a doubtful heart, but rather in the quiet assurance by faith that he'll answer us, in the best way, and at the appropriate time, because his way is perfect (Psalm 18:31).

The Lord's first followers said: "Lord, teach us to pray." In response the Lord gave them an example of praying with six major points: "Our Father who is in heaven, Hallowed be Your name. Your kingdom come. Your will be done, on earth as it is in heaven. Give us this day our daily bread. And forgive us our debts, as we also have forgiven our debtors. And do not lead us into temptation, but deliver us from evil" (Matthew 6:9-13). We might expect at any one time to major on perhaps only two or three of these points as the Holy Spirit leads us.

"Our Father in heaven" it begins, which at once reminds us that we're on the earth and God's in heaven. But this is an approach to God that's based on relationship. This form of address captures the intimacy of a child's relationship with its parent, and the bold asking which that can lead to, but without any undue familiarity. This is the intimate reverence of the adoring child of God, coming in a spirit of awe and worship. Of the six points in this model prayer the first three are most definitely God-centred - dealing with God's name, God's kingdom and God's will. We could hardly be reminded more forcibly that true prayer is a concern for the glory of God.

It isn't first and foremost about me getting my needs met, but about me giving God his rightful place. And when I give God his rightful place, then I'm put in my true place as I humble myself, and through prayer, express my total dependence on God in all his sovereignty over my life. This prayer acknowledges that God's on the throne - and he's holy. The first point made in the prayer is "Hallowed be Your Name". The Bible reminds us elsewhere that holy and reverend is God's name, and we want it to be displayed that way by the way we live: "to live more nearly as we pray", as one hymn-writer has put it.

Then the words "Your will be done" seem to cause confusion today. Some people appear to use them at the conclusion of a specific request almost as though they were a kind of "face-saver" just in case the desired result doesn't materialize. Others wonder why we need to bother to pray at all if God's going to do what he wants anyway. His will is sovereign after all, isn't it? But these words really teach us that the bottom line of all our praying has got to be: "Do what you want in my life, LORD". The essence of prayer is not me bending his will to mine, but it's about me bowing my will to his. Real prayer takes place when we plead in the power of the Spirit for what God desires. That requires that we be in tune with God, of course.

We understand prayer best, I believe, when we understand it to be a response to his initiative. He hears and acts when our prayer is according to his will. And his Spirit moves his children into the current of God's will as they spend time in prayer.

CHAPTER SIX: WONDERING ABOUT WATER BAPTISM?

The words "baptism" and "baptize" appear frequently in the New Testament. But to what do they refer? The answers often given to this question reveal a wide range of opinions. The Lord Jesus Christ said to the Father: "Your word is truth" (John 17:17). So, if we wish to know the truth about baptism, we'll have to look for it in the Bible ...

In the Acts of the Apostles chapters 2, 8, 9, 10, 16, 18 & 19, we read about people who were baptized. In each case, they were born-again believers who'd already received the good news of salvation proclaimed to them by the apostles and others. We don't read anywhere in the New Testament about infants being baptized. Baptism is only for those who personally believe in Christ, and have accepted him as their Saviour.

How is baptism to be performed? The Lord used a word that means dipping or plunging or immersing in a fluid. So, when the Lord's disciples were given the command to baptize other people, he meant for them to be plunged or dipped or immersed in water - just as he himself was immersed in the waters of the Jordan River – before being quickly brought up again. It actually says of the time when Philip baptized an Ethiopian, that "they both went down into the water." Then, as if to emphasize the immersion feature, it says: "when they came up out of the water ..." (Acts 8:38-39).

Christian baptism, by this means, is designed to symbolize burial and rising again, as explained by the Bible's explicit teaching concerning baptism. In Romans 6:4, for example, the Apostle Paul clarifies its spiritual meaning. He says, "Therefore we have been buried with Him through baptism into death, so that as Christ was raised from the dead through the glory of the Father, so we too might walk in newness of life." What's the spiritual reality which lies behind this? Well, when a person believes in Christ, God regards him or her as having died in a spiritual sense with respect to sin (Romans 6:11), the law (Galatians 2:19) and the world (Galatians 6:15). That person is now joined to the glorified and risen Christ and should live in the joy and power of the resurrection. This is what is symbolized in the act of baptism and so that act requires a burial and a resurrection.

Why should we be baptized? Is it necessary to maintain our salvation from eternal condemnation? NO. Does it make our salvation more secure? NO. Why baptism then? In addition to the meaningful symbolism already mentioned, we should also be baptized simply because it's a commandment of our Lord, to whom all authority has been given. Our motivation for being baptized will be because, since we truly love the Lord Jesus, we therefore want to obey his commands (see John 14:15).

Baptism is an important step on the path of discipleship. There are other important steps. This becomes apparent as we explore the Acts of the Apostles. There it can be seen that after baptism, the disciples were added to the existing local church. They were added to the Lord and to those who were already gathered together on the authority of the Lord. At Pentecost, all those baptized were added to the church of God in Jerusalem. It's the same today - a believer should be added to a biblical church of God.

But let's be clear, baptism is not necessary for salvation itself. Baptism is something we do; it's a work, and so it cannot save us, as the Bible plainly teaches we're not saved by works. In the second verse of the 6th chapter of Romans, Paul begins by saying ... "By no means! How can we who died to sin still live in it?" This is the basis of Paul's rejection of a "we may as well live as we please" type of philosophy. He tells them that the reality is that the believer on the Lord Jesus Christ has in fact "died to sin." But what does this mean? Let's try to understand it from what follows. In Romans 6, Paul also tells us that "Christ died to sin."

There must be a consistency between what it means for Christ to die to sin, and what it means for the believer on Christ to die to sin - since both these expressions are used in the same place in our Bible. Paul is actually explaining what it means for us to die to sin by stating that Christ died to sin while talking about our identification with Christ. That is, Paul reasons that, if Christ died to sin, and we're identified with Christ, then it follows that we, too, died to sin – and as a practical consequence it would be out of place for us to now lead a life that was dominated by sinful practices. That's the sense of the flow of this paragraph in our Bibles.

And to prove that we've been identified with Christ, Paul shares two things: a revelation of what happened at our conversion, and an explanation of the meaning of our water baptism. These two things are linked by this thought of our being identified with Christ. It's at salvation, when by God's grace we are saved through faith, that we're identified with the Christ of the cross in his death and resurrection. When we believe, it's as if Christ's death becomes our death and it's then that we receive new life in Christ. Later, in water baptism we demonstrate that fact by "acting it out" – i.e., being buried in water and rising again. Water baptism is only a symbolic witness to all who watch it taking place. We're testifying to the faith which has already saved us – so our water baptism is in effect a drama about our previous identification with a crucified and resurrected Saviour.

We should reflect meaningfully on our baptism. The Apostle Peter, describes this as "the interrogation of our conscience" (1 Peter 3:21). This might mean we ask ourselves questions like "should I go there as a baptised disciple of the Lord Jesus?" Staying true to our commitment in baptism will save our lives from corrupting influences. Only in this sense can baptism be said to "save us." In believers' baptism we make a visible, public statement of the unseen faith that's in our heart, and which has already saved us.

It's as if we're telling all those who are there to witness the event that we're under new management. We're displaying our new Christian identity as being no longer "in Adam", but now "in Christ". Baptism shows our intention to live – or walk, in the old Bible language – to walk in that newness of life – the new life we received when we first believed in Christ. At salvation, the Bible reveals to us that our former self died with Christ, and we became a new person, effective from the time of our conversion.

So then, if we live true to our baptism, day by day, we'll want to be conscious of putting away old behaviours and vices, and living a new quality of life for the Lord. In our water baptism, we've a reminder about our need to display our new Christian identity as a disciple of Jesus Christ even as we grow and mature spiritually. We also declare our commitment to live for the Saviour who died for us. I once heard my friend Ed tell a true story about the type of commitment involved in following Christ. In Israel one day, Ed was talking to an Israeli helicopter pilot. The pilot told him how he'd been involved in an accident. His helicopter had flown too near the side-wall of the valley or chasm, and one of the rotors had struck the rocks. It had come crashing out of the sky. The pilot had survived, obviously, but one of the rotors had almost sliced his leg off. The surgeon had wanted to amputate it, saying it was so badly damaged it would be useless. But the pilot had begged that he be allowed to keep his leg.

As soon as he was able, he got a bicycle and strapped his dead leg to one pedal, and pedalled away with his good leg. He did this day after day for a long, long time. Slowly, his damaged leg began to gain power, and he was able to rejoin active service. While he was standing talking to Ed, his alarm sounded. Duty was calling. At that very moment, his presence was required in the air due to some threat against Israel's borders. Ed says that man ran across the car park to his helicopter: and then he added "now that's what I call commitment!"

Jesus Christ says in Luke 9:23: "If anyone wishes to come after Me, he must deny himself, and take up his cross daily and follow Me. Baptism is the way to begin to show that same calibre of commitment to the cause of Christ. But as well as **displaying our Christian identity**; and as well as **declaring our commitment** to follow the Lord Jesus; believers' baptism also **demonstrates our love** for the Saviour who first loved us. Jesus said in John 14:15: "If you love Me, you will keep My commandments. And then the Lord commanded his first disciples in Matthew 28:19-20 to: "Go … and make disciples of all the nations, baptizing them in the name of the Father and the Son and the Holy Spirit, teaching them to observe all that I commanded you."

And they did that, for as we've seen Paul commanded unbaptized believers to be baptized in the name of the Lord Jesus, the single name of the triune God. When we keep this command, like any other, we show our love to the Lord. In that sense baptism becomes a test of our love for the Son of God who loved us and gave himself for us (Galatians 2:20).

I remember hearing about an unusual test of love. A certain Lieutenant Blandford had taken a book from among the hundreds of Army library books at his Florida training camp. In it, he discovered handwritten notes in a woman's writing. Her name was written at the front too: it was Hollis Meynell. So he'd got hold of a New York City telephone book and found her address. He'd written, and she'd answered. Next day he'd been shipped out, but they'd gone on writing. When, at last, home from his tour of duty, he arranged to be standing under the clock at the Grand Central Station in New York, waiting for his first meeting with Hollis Meynell whom he was to recognize by the red rose she'd be wearing in her lapel. At one minute to six, he noticed a young woman coming toward him. Dressed in a green suit, her figure was long and slim; her blond hair lay back in curls, her eyes blue as flowers. He started toward her ... it was then he saw Hollis Meynell. She was standing almost directly behind the girl, a woman well past 40, her greying hair tucked under a worn hat. She was more than plump; her thick-ankled feet were thrust into low-heeled shoes. But she wore a red rose in the rumpled lapel of her brown coat. Blandford felt as though he were being split in two, so keen was his desire to follow the girl in green, yet so deep was his longing for the woman whose spirit had truly upheld his own. Her pale, plump face was gentle and sensible; he could see that now. Her grey eyes had a warm, kindly twinkle. This would be something perhaps even rarer than love.

He squared his broad shoulders, saluted and said: "I'm Lieutenant John Blandford, and you - you must be Miss Meynell. I'm so glad you could meet me. May I take you to dinner?" The woman's face broadened in a tolerant smile. "I don't know what this is all about, son," she answered. "That young lady in the green suit - the one who just went by - begged me to wear this rose on my coat. And she said that if you asked me to go out with you, I should tell you that she's waiting for you in that big restaurant across the street. She said it was some kind of a test."

We can think of baptism as a test. Since it's a command of the Lord Jesus, whether we submit to water baptism or not is really his test of the reality of our love for him. May I ask: "Have you proved and demonstrated your love; have you declared your commitment; and have you displayed your Christian identity – all by going through the waters of baptism? No? – then what's hindering you?

CHAPTER SEVEN: DISCOVERING THE BIBLE'S PATTERN FOR SERVICE

Have you ever noticed the precise sequencing of branches and leaves in a simple plant such as the one known as the sneezewort? If you count the number of branches at successive levels, you'll discover the numbers follow what's known as the Fibonacci sequence, with each number formed by the addition of the two previous numbers in sequence. Observing a pattern like that makes the tasks of recognition, memory and description a whole lot easier.

The Bible isn't as difficult to understand once we begin to see that it, too, contains a pattern – in fact it emphasizes a repeated feature of patterns. In the natural world, when we model some dynamic situations mathematically – like the ever-changing size of a population - we get representations of reality where repeated patterns show the existence of a larger structure, worth studying. And it's the repetition of features in the Bible that invites us to expect to find a prescribed pattern in the historical descriptions of early Christian practices.

People "do church" in different ways today. One way is to recognize that the first apostolic churches of which we read in the New Testament supply us with a pattern which it's intended that we should follow exactly in every generation. All other ways of "doing Christianity" is to read the same texts, but to see them as providing underlying principles for different creative adaptations in all subsequent times. Some of these ways may resemble the first way in parts, but it's not really about comparing parts but rather the sum of the parts. The key question is: "Is there, or is there not, a pattern to be followed?"

Paul says: "... knowing this, that our old self was crucified with Him, in order that our body of sin might be done away with, so that we would no longer be slaves to sin; Even so consider yourselves to be dead to sin, but alive to God in Christ Jesus. Therefore do not let sin reign in your mortal body so that you obey its lusts, and do not go on presenting the members of your body to sin as instruments of unrighteousness; but present yourselves to God as those alive from the dead, and your members as instruments of righteousness to God. Do you not know that when you present yourselves to someone as slaves for obedience, you are slaves of the one whom you obey, either of sin resulting in death, or of obedience resulting in righteousness? But thanks be to God that though you were slaves of sin, you became obedient from the heart to that form of teaching to which you were committed, and having been freed from sin, you became slaves of righteousness" (Romans 6:6,11-13, 16-18).

These verses follow from the Apostle Paul's explanation of believer's water baptism as being our symbolic identification with Christ in his death, burial and resurrection. Paul goes on to explain the reason for this symbolism is the reality that Christ's death was our death: Christ was serving the death sentence which our sins deserved. Now united with Christ through our faith, we're no longer the same person we once were. We have a new Christian identity, and the freedom to express it in new Christian behaviours. "Don't live as you lived before you knew Christ" is Paul's basic message in Romans chapter 6. We're no longer to obey sinful desires in the way we employ the members of our body – what we watch, where we go etc. – but we're to do what's right by obeying what Paul describes literally as "the pattern of teaching".

This pattern was, of course, the Lord's own, later communicated by his apostles, and now contained through their writings within the New Testament Scriptures. So in our new life as a baptised disciple, the Lord intends we should serve him by following the pattern he's given us.

The Bible repeatedly mentions the existence of a pattern to be followed by those who served God at different time points in history throughout the progressive revelation of God that's shared in the Bible. Take Moses for example, who was told by God: "see to it that you make them [the furnishings of God's special tent or house] according to the pattern which was shown you on the mountain" (Exodus 25:40). The fact that this was important to God – the fact that his people should serve according to God's own pattern - is confirmed by its repetition to Moses on two further occasions (Exodus 26:30; 27:8); and then it's additionally referred to by the Holy Spirit on another three occasions later on in the Bible (Numbers 8:4; Acts 7:44; Hebrews 8:5). And on into the New Testament, the apostles pick up on this critical point, with Paul saying to Timothy, "hold fast to the pattern of sound words" (2 Timothy 1:13).

How was that pattern for Christian service expressed in the first century? Well, the big picture – the overall picture - is of a company of disciples, all baptized by immersion in water, all added locally to church of God fellowship, all within an overall community serving according to one pattern of teaching everywhere, maintained under a fellowship of elders and separated to God.

Here we see biblical church fellowship, and the biblical fellowship of churches. Consistent with the picture or pattern we've just outlined from the pages of the Bible, let's now pick out some specifics: there was only ever one church in each town or city; in it only baptized and added believers were received to share in the Breaking of the Bread. And addition to one of the local churches, effectively meant addition to all of them because of their connectional nature. These first century churches, known simply as churches of God, were coordinated by means of there being a group of elders in each one and these elders consulted with those in the other churches on issues affecting all the churches.

In this way, the individual churches of God were not autonomous or independent but rather – in the Bible phrase – 'fitly framed together' with the resulting united or interdependent structure being described in the New Testament as God's temple or house on earth. In aggregate then, the first century churches of God answered to the tabernacle tent of Moses' time, or the temple of Solomon's era. This New Testament spiritual house for God to reside in on earth was composed of all the churches of God seen together, and united in their service. The clue we pick up from all that precedes this in the Old Testament indicates that this description of what they did is one which God definitely intends to be prescriptive.

Recently in the U.K., DNA testing was used to verify remains as being those of King Richard III. In much the same way, we can compare the spiritual strands of modern church structures with the biblical blueprint – even stretching back into the Old Testament - to check for biblical authenticity. In the background of the Old Testament, the children of Abraham from whom God's people were called to a life of obedience in a covenant relationship from which they could be 'cut off' – albeit they could never lose their racial place as a child of Abraham. And in the New Testament, 'the Church which is his [Christ's] Body' (Ephesians 1:22,23) is comparable to Abraham's descendants as the 'pool' from which God's obedient people are gathered, and from that gathered people they can, sadly, be ex-communicated (e.g. 1

Corinthians 5:13) – although never losing their place as a child of God in the Body of Christ.

At the highest level of comparison, we observe that God's people in both Testaments were saved by blood, baptized in water, and obeyed the teaching of the Lord for their respective time. What's more, God's house in any biblical age has always been the place where God resides and rests among those who continue to follow his rules. And God's priesthood has always been those privileged to draw near to God's presence in prescribed sanctuary worship. And God's holy nation may always be identified as those united with an identifying citizenship and with exclusive boundaries. Finally, God's kingdom is consistently in every age where God rules by his Word over his people.

In Exodus 19:5,6; 25:8 we read: "... if you will indeed obey My voice ... then you shall be My own possession among all the peoples, for all the earth is Mine; and you shall be to Me a kingdom of priests and a holy nation ... Let them construct a sanctuary for Me, that I may dwell among them." And alongside that, in 1 Peter 2:5,9 we read: "You ... are being built up as a spiritual house for a holy priesthood ... a chosen race, a royal priesthood, a holy nation, a people for God's own possession."

Clearly these same "entities" (of a people, kingdom, priesthood, holy nation and house) are revealed in both the Old and New Testaments. In Exodus 24, they were established by the Old Covenant. In the New Testament, their sequels are established by the New Covenant (the "sprinkled ... blood", 1 Peter 1:2). Their expression may be intermittent, partial, and flawed, but they can only be claimed by those building on the same basis as the Apostles once built. Believers who build today on the same constitutional basis as the first believers: those who build carefully on the same pattern or mould of teaching (Romans 6:17; 2 Timothy 1:13) are able to make the claim that the same results materialise as in the first century when they simply use the same mould.

When the same pattern is taught, as when builders follow the same architectural drawings at a different time, what emerges can be described in exactly the same terms as anything previously constructed using the same drawings. Let me try to explain it in another way. You've heard it said that it's a mark of insanity when someone repeatedly does the same thing and expects to get a different result (like trying the wrong key in a lock); but then equally, is it not entirely rational to do exactly the same as was done 2,000 years ago and expect, indeed claim, to get the same result?

When each part of the Bible, understood in a certain way, builds up into a coherent overall view, then we have confirmation of our understanding of each part and we can defend against the challenge 'Oh, that's just your interpretation of that particular verse.'

BONUS CHAPTER ONE: KNOWING CHRIST

The basin and the towel must have condemned the hearts of the twelve men who entered the upper room that night with the Lord Jesus. None of the disciples were prepared to reach for these objects and perform the humble task of washing the feet of the others. They had been arguing among themselves about who was the greatest, so none of them would lower themselves just at that moment. Then a shocking thing happened ...

In a move that seems to symbolize how the Lord laid aside his heavenly glory and stooped to gird himself with humanity, He, their Lord and Master, took the towel and basin and began to make his way around the group, washing their feet. Amazingly, this would become the one recorded moment in the Gospels when the Lord affirmed the disciples' declaration that He was their Lord (John 13:13)! The reality of His lordship, and the glory of His leadership, was revealed in that lowly act of service. Perhaps it was Peter's guilty conscience that led him to protest against the Lord of glory stooping to wash his feet. Christ's reply was pregnant with meaning: "What I do you do not realize now, but you will understand hereafter" (John 13:7). That statement drew a fine distinction between two different kinds of knowledge. The sense of the Lord's remark was that Peter could not then perceive by observation the significance of the Lord's action; but, rather, that he would come to know much more of it through experience.

"The only thing wrong with experience", someone has quipped, "is that it comes at the wrong end of life!" That's probably the impatient view of a generation that wants instant results, but in human experience there can be no instant maturity. Later in the

Bible, when the disciple Peter counselled younger men - in all likelihood younger church leaders – to "clothe themselves with humility" (1 Peter 5:5), can it seriously be doubted that the upper room incident was clearly in his mind? By then he'd come to know the true meaning of the Lord's breath-taking act which had cut through the sullen atmosphere among the disciples on that, for them, shameful night. By means of the experience of the Holy Spirit residing in him since that first Pentecost, Peter had grown in his relationship with the Lord Jesus, and now delighted in the humble mind of Christ. The Lord's promise about Peter coming to know the significance of the feet-washing that night in the upper room had been fulfilled. This had indeed been something learnt later through experience.

This knowledge that's gained through experience often implies a relationship with the person that's being known; in fact, it's usually a relationship in which the person or thing becomes more and more valued. Peter had certainly come to value that amazing object lesson in humility and applied its significance to himself and also to others. In the seventh verse of John chapter 14, the Lord again contrasted these two different types of knowledge when he replied to Thomas: "If you had known Me (by experience), you would have known My Father (by observation)".

As we've already commented, the type of knowledge that's gained through experience usually involves a growing relationship with, and a developing appreciation of, the person or thing that's being known. Of course, that's how it's meant to be with our knowing Christ. If the quality of the relationship Thomas and the other disciples had experienced with Christ had been all that it might have been, then the Lord said that they could have clearly observed in him the true character of the Father as faithfully displayed in the Son.

The apostle Paul takes up this idea of knowing from experience and uses it in his Bible letters to capture something of the essence of his deep longing to know Christ. You just need to read one of Paul's letters (for example, his letter to the Philippians) to see that getting to know Christ better and better - through ever closer experience - was the steady pursuit of Paul's life. For him, Christianity was first and foremost a relationship with Jesus Christ. For each of us, too, the Christian life is to be a rich experience of knowing Christ. Paul shares with us at a very personal level in the third chapter of his letter to the Philippians. He explains that for him, since getting to know Christ, everything else in life had lost its value and had become totally eclipsed by the surpassing value of knowing Christ. Knowledge like this is knowledge of something we've really come to value. For Paul, everything that had once been gain to him or that he'd valued in his life at one time, now paled totally into insignificance compared with the wonder of knowing Christ. This was the object of supreme value now in Paul's life. This is how he puts it:

"But what things were gain to me, these I have counted loss for Christ. Yet indeed I also count all things loss for the excellence of the knowledge of Christ Jesus my Lord, for whom I have suffered the loss of all things, and count them as rubbish, that I may know Him and the power of His resurrection, and the fellowship of His sufferings, being conformed to His death" (Philippians 3:7-10).

This is Paul's pursuit of a lifetime. His longing is to know the heart and will of Christ through close association. For Paul, to be in this relationship with Christ is all about knowing him and becoming more like him. This desire which Paul has for himself is something he longs that others might share as well. When he prays for his friends at Philippi, he asks: "that your love may abound still more and more in knowledge" (Philippians 1:9). Abounding 'more and more in knowledge' is at the heart of the abundant life that Christ came to give us.

But it's worth noting that Paul has sharpened things up even further here. This is the word for getting to know through experience, but it's got something else added to it. The added prefix has the effect of implying knowledge that's more specialized and particular. Paul's use of this word, under the Spirit's guidance, hints at a still more advanced knowledge. Recognising this, the translators of our Bibles often describe it in terms of real knowledge or full knowledge or even exact knowledge.

There's a famous Bible passage in 1 Corinthians chapter 13 that illustrates this further difference very well. It's there that Paul contrasts our present, partial and experiential knowledge with that future time at the coming of the Lord when we'll know then as fully as we ourselves are known. With all these shades of meaning available in the New Testament language, and the Holy Spirit's choice being, as we can be sure, a very deliberate one, it can only be helpful to focus on three main passages where the idea of full or exact knowledge is distinctively used. Paul uses it in Colossians chapter 2 verse 2, when praying for his friends in the Churches of God at Colossae and at Laodicea. He frames his prayer in terms of their finding encouragement in the full assurance of a true knowledge of Christ. Paul seems to be expressing the conviction that there was a particular appreciation of Christ - a particular way of relating to him - that ought to characterize the believers in those New Testament churches of God.

We might ask: "What exactly was that?" Paul expands on this same word in his opening chapter addressed to the Church of God at Ephesus. Again it's contained in his prayer for them: "that the God of our Lord Jesus Christ, the Father of glory, may give to you the spirit of wisdom and revelation in the knowledge of Him, the eyes of your understanding being enlightened; that you may know what is the hope of His calling, what are the riches of the glory of His inheritance in the saints, and what is the exceeding greatness of His power toward us who believe, according to the working of His mighty power" (Ephesians 1:17-19).

This particular knowledge is appropriate to those whose relationship with Christ is bound up with an appreciation of God's call, and with God's present inheritance in Churches of God, and with God's great power. This knowledge of Christ, as Paul himself defines it, is a specific revelation of Christ encompassing God's view of the Churches of God, the Church of God at Ephesus being one among them at that time. His prayer for these Ephesian believers was that their evaluation of their place in their local church of God ought to flow out from their particular appreciation of Christ. All these churches planted or visited or cared for by Paul were integrated into the one community of "companions" or "fellows" of Christ (Hebrews 1:9).

Companying with him and knowing him in the experience of Christian fellowship was the very core of life in these New Testament churches. Indeed, it was what united them, as Paul remarks in Ephesians chapter 4, commenting on the unity of the faith and of the knowledge of the Son of God (v.13). The fact that the unity existing throughout disciples in the various New Testament churches of God is described as "the unity of the knowledge of the Son of God" is a very remarkable thing.

Their unity was characterized not only by a common adherence to the authentic Faith or body of Christian doctrine - vital as that was - but it was also a unity characterized in terms of their particular appreciation of Christ. The appreciation of specific aspects of a biblical relationship with Christ ought to lead to its valued expression in churches of God. This has never appealed to me more than when teaching on the glories of Jesus as the "great priest over the house of God" (Hebrews 10:21) to Filipino friends recently gathered into a Church of God.

BONUS CHAPTER TWO: ENJOYING CHRISTIAN FELLOWSHIP

There's a hymn that begins: "Great the joy when Christians meet; Christian fellowship how sweet". Many would no doubt echo these sentiments but, when it comes down to it, what do we actually mean by "fellowship"? Perhaps the idea of fellowship conjures up the idea of sharing tea and biscuits over a chat. But the qualifier "Christian" fellowship implies that the basis of that fellowship is our shared experience of Christ. The first Bible mention of Christian fellowship (the Greek word used in the New Testament is "koinonia") is in Acts chapter 2.

There's a very special and historic reason for our being introduced to the subject there. For that's where we find the record of the descent from heaven of the Holy Spirit. From that point in time, fifty days after Jesus' resurrection, the Helper the Lord had promised came to take up residence in the hearts of all born-again believers in this present Church Age. Having the Spirit of Christ in our lives is essential to any experience of Christian fellowship. We may have been attracted to the company of believers who were demonstrating Christian qualities in their relationships with each other before we ourselves became Christians, but our personal participation in true Christian fellowship can only date from the time in our own experience when the Holy Spirit came to take up residence in our lives.

This Bible word which translates as "fellowship" basically means a joint participation together in something of mutual interest. In a Christian context, those common interests are the interests of Jesus Christ himself (Philippians 2:21). It's those interests which the Holy Spirit advances in our lives as believers. Having noticed the necessary connection between the coming of the Holy Spirit and the first mention of Christian fellowship, let's turn now to the benediction with which the apostle Paul closes the second of his two letters to the Church of God at Corinth: "The grace of our Lord Jesus Christ, and the love of God, and the fellowship of the Holy Spirit, be with you all" (2 Corinthians 13:14).

"The grace of the Lord Jesus be with you", Paul said to the disciples. Where did he expect the grace of the Lord Jesus to be displayed? In the disciple lives of his Corinthian friends, surely, through their gracious conduct with each other. Paul's spiritual wish was also that the love of God might be with them. How would God's love be evident? Once again, it must have been the apostle's expectation that this would be shown in the lives of the disciples. Finally, Paul expresses the longing that the fellowship of the Holy Spirit might be with them.

It doesn't seem reasonable that this should be translated as "fellowship with the Holy Spirit"; but since the subject of the benediction was the grace of the Lord Jesus Christ and the love of God, this also properly refers to the fellowship of the Holy Spirit. And it was to be demonstrated in the same way as the grace and love, that is in the lives of the disciples as they fellowshipped together with each other. Their joint participation in things of mutual interest would derive from the Holy Spirit himself.

So, mutual interest in the things of Jesus Christ, an interest stemming from the Holy Spirit within each disciple, would lead to their joint participation in these things in a harmonious way. This kind of unity is once again what Paul describes at the end of Philippians chapter 1 and the beginning of Philippians chapter 2 - the very section in which Paul again mentions the "fellowship of the Spirit" (2:1). Spirit-produced fellowship brings about unity between Christians.

The fellowship of the united churches of God that's so amply demonstrated in the New Testament is listed alongside the apostles' teaching in Acts 2, verses 41 and 42 - the earliest believers being said to continue steadfastly in the fellowship and in the apostles' teaching. The relationship between them is perhaps brought out most clearly by the apostle John in the first of his letters. He writes to the end that believers might enjoy fellowship with them: that is, with the apostles who had been companions of Christ. As a basis for that fellowship, John says he's sharing "what we have seen and heard'. This was what he and the other apostles had seen of and heard from Christ - in other words the Person of Christ and his teaching which he had delivered to the apostles, and which they had made their own.

This experience of Christian fellowship was based on something more than the shared understanding of Christ's teaching ("what we have heard"). It was based also on a communication of their appreciation of Christ himself ("what we have seen"). So the apostles' fellowship was linked to the apostles' teaching and to their real experience of Christ. These were things they wished others to share in: "so that you may have fellowship with us", John the apostle writes. This offer is, of course, still open to us today by virtue of what the Holy Spirit caused the apostles to record in the New Testament Scriptures: Scriptures that are full of Christ and his commands. The apostles shared these things so that others might have fellowship with them - so that others, including ourselves today, might participate jointly in the interests of Jesus Christ.

"The interests of Jesus Christ" is an expression drawn from the Philippians' letter. Paul was writing disappointedly of believers whose chief concern was their own interests, he says, not the interests of Jesus Christ. But, he tells us, Timothy was different. He had Christ's interests at heart. This was said to be demonstrated by his concern for the welfare of those in the church of God at Philippi (2:20-21). From this we can learn of the deep interest of Jesus Christ in churches of God as we find them biblically defined in New Testament times. Our sharing fellowship with the apostles is a sharing fellowship with the Father and the Son. John says, so that you may have fellowship with us; and our fellowship is with the Father, and with His Son.

This fellowship can be richly experienced by all who, like Timothy, enter into the active interest Jesus Christ had in churches of God. After all, this is what the apostles, at the Lord's command, devoted themselves to furthering. As we've noted from the first letter of John, the apostles' fellowship was a fellowship of Christ - sharing what they'd seen of and heard from him. The call to every Christian is a call to be a "fellow of Christ". Certainly, that was the calling of Hebrew believers, Jewish Christians, in the first churches of God.

The writer to the Hebrews, in the first chapter, describes the Lord Jesus as being anointed with the oil of gladness above his "companions" or his "fellows". But who were these fellows of Christ? One Bible scholar (W.E. Vine) has deduced from scripture that being a fellow of Christ marks an even closer relationship than being a brother of Christ. Christ is not ashamed to call all members of his Church "brothers". How special is that! And yet it's suggested that to be a fellow or companion of Christ is something even closer in terms of relationship. In the early days of Christianity, believers like those mentioned, found themselves in churches of God. But the time came when, under the pressure of persecution, some Jewish believers were considering turning back or falling away from their new-found Christian identity in churches of God and going back to the old ways of Judaism. A lot of the language of the Hebrews' letter is aimed at pleading with its first readers to hold fast and not to fall away. But they couldn't fall away from the relation of being a brother to Christ (one of his brethren).

Nowhere, when rightly understood in context, does the Bible teach our eternal security in Christ is ever in any doubt. In contrast, the first letter to the Corinthians makes clear that an immoral brother was put away from the local church of God fellowship at Corinth. The Hebrew Christians too, were in danger of losing their place in the fellowship of the churches of God. When the writer wants to impress on them something of the enormity of such a backsliding decision, he contrasts Israel's Old Testament calling with the Hebrews' New Testament calling.

The call of God to his people Israel was an earthly calling - one which called them to an earthly country and a sanctuary of this world. The New Testament call described in Hebrews is, by contrast, a heavenly calling. These Hebrews in the early community of Churches of God in the first century were, Hebrews chapter 3 verse 1 says, "sharers or fellows of a heavenly calling". How could they even consider not holding fast to the privilege of being companions of Christ and being sharers of that better heavenly calling?

Verse 14 of chapter 3 in Hebrews impresses on these early Christians the vital need to hold onto their Christian confidence if they were to avoid losing this relationship of being "partakers or fellows of Christ". If they chose to exit from obedience to the apostolic Faith, if they gave up on continuing steadfastly in the New Testament churches of God, then they would fall away from this close relationship. This danger of falling away is time and again brought before the readers of this Bible letter. Again we say that it's made abundantly clear in many ways throughout the New Testament that we can't fall away from the Body of Christ; but there's evidently something we can fall away from. We can fall away from the fellowship belonging to God's Son, the Lord Jesus Christ.

As fellows of the heavenly calling, they had been called into the fellowship into which disciples began to enter in Acts chapter 2:42. In churches of God patterned after the first Church of God at Jerusalem, they all belonged to the overall fellowship belonging to God's Son (1 Corinthians 1:9). The theme of the Hebrews' letter with its stress on 'fellows of Christ' is that of a worshipping people, a kingdom of priests on earth which serves God with a heavenly calling by entering the true holy place in heaven to worship now through Jesus as "great priest over the house of God" (Hebrews 10:21). That's where this subject of fellowship leads us to!

BONUS CHAPTER THREE: BEING CHRISTLIKE

It's possible that the upper room setting for Jesus' final teaching session with his disciples was a room with a view over one of the valleys surrounding Jerusalem. But as his followers filed into the room on the evening before he was due to die, they may well have wondered what their future prospects would be, especially when the Lord began to make plain to them the fact of his imminent departure. We can imagine how they would have reacted to that news. They'd left everything behind to follow him; they'd become so dependent on him day by day; and now he was leaving them. So why wouldn't their outlook appear bleak? Perhaps, this wasn't a room with a view after all? To address their fears that evening, the Lord opened various "windows" for them through his teaching ministry. The things he taught them gave them a view of what it would be like for them after he had returned to heaven.

One of those "views" which I'd like us to consider, was the prospect of Christlikeness; that is, the prospect of followers of Christ actually becoming like Christ. Here are some of the Lord's words to his followers that evening in the upper room (from John 17). Notice how they open a window for us onto the idea of being like Christ: "Now I am no longer in the world, but these are in the world, and I come to You. Holy Father, keep through Your name those whom You have given Me, that they may be one as We are" (v.11).

The very first thing we can see from this is that, by remaining together as his followers, they'd be sharing likeness to Christ in unity. More was to follow as Christ continued in prayer for them:

"But now I come to You, and these things I speak in the world, that they may have My joy fulfilled in themselves." (v.13) Christ's request here makes it very clear that his left-behind followers were to experience joy - and that joy was to be his very own joy. Jesus' joy on earth had been to do his Father's will. Now they, too, were to share likeness to Christ by doing God's will on earth with joy. Then the Lord continued further in His prayer to the Father: "Sanctify them by Your truth. Your word is truth. As You sent Me into the world, I also have sent them into the world" (v.17-18). It was the Lord's desire that their sending out in mission work was to be modelled on his own sending: when his Father had sent him into the world. They were to share likeness to Christ in consecrated commissioning. Finally, the Lord prayed: "And the glory which You gave Me I have given them, that they may be one just as We are one" (v.22).

So his glory was to be seen in them. In the Lord's plan, they were to share likeness to Christ in glory, glorifying God in all their service for him. It's really exciting that this is God's plan for us, too - exactly the same! It hasn't changed. The Lord's view from the upper room was a long view, right down the corridors of time. The far-sighted Saviour also had twenty-first century disciples in view. He made that clear in verse twenty, when he said, "I do not pray for these alone, but also for those who will believe in Me through their word."

The Saviour saw his followers spreading out into all the world after his death and resurrection, taking with them the Christian message. He looked forward to his own likeness becoming apparent in every place where New Testament Churches of God came into existence. They would be all linked to each other, just as long before in the days of Moses individual curtains had been linked together to form a special tent of curtains, known as the Tabernacle, in which God lived among his people's tents in the desert. Let's stay with that thought for a moment, for it illustrates for us the kind of unity Christ was praying for among his followers. Those curtains which were linked together to form God's house on earth long ago were all made to the one identical design and pattern - which you can read about in Exodus chapter 26.

It's biblical to think of God's house on earth today being made up of disciples in churches of God. There's no doubting that was the case in New Testament times when churches like the Church of God at Corinth and the Church of God at Jerusalem and the Church of God at Ephesus formed one interlinked church Fellowship which was where God lived on earth in and through his Holy Spirit. Those individual churches were like the individual but identically designed Tabernacle curtains. What's more, the curtains of the Tabernacle were made to be like the veil which was hung up inside it. And the letter to the Hebrews informs us that the veil pictured the Lord Jesus himself. So that's interesting, for as the curtains were to be like the veil, we now find Christ praying that his disciples might be like him, the true veil. As disciples, we're to be like Christ in our attitude (Philippians 2) and in our behaviour (1 John 2:6). You may say: "How can we do that?" The Bible counsels us to "put on Christ" (Galatians 3:27), and talks very specifically of "learning Christ" (Ephesians 4:21); obeying Christ; "abiding in Christ" (1 John 2:6); and "imitating Christ" (1 Corinthians 11:1). By way of these disciplines, in Bible-based communion, our characters are to be transformed through the Holy Spirit's work (2 Corinthians 3:17-18), making us to be meek and lowly in our attitude just as Christ was; and forgiving and loving in our behaviour too.

By sharing likeness to Christ in unity as disciples, it's also God's desire that we share likeness to his Son in the joyful fulfilment of divine purpose. That his own joy might be fulfilled in us was the Saviour's own longing for us that night in the upper room - sharers of his joy, in that way becoming like him. It's beautiful, isn't it? Christ's joy was in doing his Father's will, no doubt about that. The line of the hymn captures the challenge for us: "Our joy to do the Father's will".

The apostle Paul later linked joy with "progress in the faith" (Philippians 1). Going forward in obedience to Christ's teaching – which was given through his apostles - is to be a pathway to increasing joy in service. The joy of Christ as the Sent One is something we can experience in a real way as we share likeness to Christ in his consecrated commission. It's his expressed desire, expressed as we've seen in the upper room that night, that we be sent out into the world by him, in the same way as he was sent by his Father into the world. As with the Master, so it has to be with the servant. But how was he sent? Let's allow the Bible to answer that from John chapter 10:36). He was the One "whom the Father sanctified and sent into the world".

So, how was he sent? As One who was sanctified or consecrated: in other words set apart to the will of God in his life. As we share likeness to Christ in consecrated service, we too are to be sanctified by the Word of God. Our mission and our ministry are to be Bible-based. One reason why Christ went to the cross was to consecrate the biblical pattern for how we serve God together unitedly as Christ's disciples.

When we do things God's way, he's glorified. It's the final way we can think of sharing likeness to Christ, for his entire life of service glorified God. God's glory was seen in that house of curtains long ago. In the same way, the heart of God is looking for biblical churches of God today, linked together in the way he designed and consecrated so that he may be glorified as he lives down here on earth among united disciples. May our paths be ordered as Christ's were, ordered in a divine unity to the glory of God. It's a unity associated with glory – his glory. What a prospect from the upper room window after all! What a prospect to share likeness to Christ in glory, in mission, in joy and in unity!

BONUS CHAPTER FOUR: WALKING THE WAY OF LOVE

Among the ruins of ancient Corinth today - and popular with bus parties of tourists - stands a marble block known as St. Paul's Polyglot bearing the "Inscription of the Hymn of Love". On it are engraved the words of the first eight verses of 1 Corinthians chapter 13. It's a nice touch, linking the geographical location of the first century Church of God at Corinth with these words which were written to it. Let's remind ourselves of this ancient "hymn of love" which is from First Corinthians chapter 13:

"If I speak with the tongues of men and of angels, but do not have love, I have become a noisy gong or a clanging cymbal; and if I have the gift of prophecy, and know all mysteries and all knowledge; and if I have all faith, so as to remove mountains, but do not have love, I am nothing. And if I give all my possessions to feed the poor, and if I deliver my body to be burned, but do not have love, it profits me nothing. Love is patient, love is kind, and is not jealous; love does not brag and is not arrogant, does not act unbecomingly; it does not seek its own, is not provoked, does not take into account a wrong suffered, does not rejoice in unrighteousness, but rejoices with the truth; bears all things, believes all things, hopes all things, endures all things. Love never fails; but if there are gifts of prophecy, they will be done away; if there are tongues, they will cease; if there is knowledge, it will be done away. But now abide faith, hope, love, these three; but the greatest of these is love" (NASB).

I'd like us to look into the whole of the first letter Paul wrote to Corinth to see if we can find out why in particular he wrote to them in this way about love. At the end of the previous chapter he declared he was about to show them "a still more excellent way" – a more excellent way than what? I'm sure many of us have seen these words about love overprinted, not on marble perhaps, but on a photo-poster depicting a beautiful sunset, nature shot or possibly a sentimental or even romantic image. That's not, however, the biblical background for these words found in First Corinthians 13.

Their context in God's inspired Word can be traced to the competitive and divided condition of the Church of God in Corinth. Sadly there were divisions in that Church. How can Christians hope to witness to the unity of the Church which is Christ's body when different Bible teachings are set aside by each different group? Paul emphasized that unity in churches of God was an important reflection of the unity of the Body of Christ itself.

Perhaps the most serious of all divisions that existed at Corinth was the division between some of them and the apostle Paul himself. There seems to have been a false sense of "spirituality" among some of the folks at Corinth in those days. From Paul's opening words in this chapter, it seems that when they used the then current gift of tongues, they believed they were actually speaking with the tongues of angels! It's even been suggested by those who take this to be a fair assumption that it explains why some of them had written to Paul expressing their low view of marriage as well as a disturbingly casual attitude to physical relations. Angels, we recall, neither marry nor are given in marriage (Luke 20:35).

So anyone taking angels as their model of spirituality might be tempted to undervalue the sanctity of marriage. This might also have been linked to their denial of the fact that believers will be raised with a transformed physical body - which triggered Paul's brilliantly reasoned defence of the truth of bodily resurrection in chapter 15. In those days there was a heresy known as Gnosticism and, like these heretics, some of the Corinthians probably considered things to do with the body as being immaterial as far as their spirituality was concerned. That, of course, became a licence for shocking behaviour - just like the behaviour of some at Corinth.

It would be hard to prove anything, but it's at least possible that this was the kind of pagan spirituality that may have governed the mentality of some at Corinth. It's very interesting because the idea of what constitutes a person as "spiritual" is again a huge area of debate today. It throws up about as many weird and unbiblical notions now as were once found around the docks at ancient Corinth. Some Christian factions emphasize certain experiences or techniques. Others argue that one doesn't need to be a Christian in order to be spiritual, although it might help! The reading of certain texts is regarded as sacred; the participation in mind and body exercises; chants, vows, meditation and mantras are all increasingly popular, it seems. But all that is background to our subject of "the more excellent way of love" - trusting that it will throw some light on why this corrective is now applied by Paul. Chapter 13 with its "hymn of love" certainly comes in by way of being a corrective against the abuse of tongues-speaking in Corinth; but more than that, we suggest it was also a corrective against some there who were claiming that they possessed a superior kind of spirituality. This claim was promoting individualism and competition among them. No wonder Paul lays down the challenge, "if anyone thinks he is spiritual, let him recognize that the things which I write to you are the Lord's commandment" (1 Corinthians 14:37)!

From chapter twelve through chapter fourteen, Paul outlines his view of spirituality. He sees it as having to do with cultivating relationships with fellow-disciples of Christ who have been led to building each other up in local church settings. Now that, he says, is an expression of genuine Christian love. The beginning of chapter 14 connects with the end of chapter 12 and so chapter 13, the "hymn of love", forms a very relevant digression aimed at showing that it is love that edifies. Chapter 13 itself seems to fall into three parts dealing with: the necessity of love (vv. 1-3), the character of love (vv. 4-7) and the permanence of love (vv. 8-13). Let's take them in that order through the chapter.

The first three verses concentrate on the necessity of love. It's here Paul begins to describe the way that's beyond comparison. He begins with a reference to where their problem lay. Was true spirituality, even then, measured by tongues-speaking or the gift of the miraculous, or faith, or knowledge? No, says Paul, spirituality is about walking by the Spirit of God and the main ethic involved is loving one another: to be toward others in the same way as God in Christ has been towards us. In other words, such signs as mentioned at the head of the chapter are not evidence of true spirituality, but Christian love is. Verses 4 to 7, which follow, deal with the character of love. Love is characterized here by no less than 15 verbs, all explaining what love is and what it's not. Love is both patient and kind: both passive and active, as seen in God's own forbearance and intervention. It seems from the twelve preceding chapters in this letter that the negative things listed at this point are precisely what they had been guilty of at Corinth.

Love doesn't envy - remember their strife and rivalry at Corinth (1 Corinthians 3:3); as revealed by their divisions in following the different personalities? Love doesn't boast - yet they had a preference for the showy gifts. Love isn't proud or puffed up - but they had been arrogant in the face of gross sin. Love isn't rude or shameful - but the "haves" among them at Corinth had been shaming the "have-nots" at their love-feasts. Love isn't self-seeking - but some of them had been stumbling others by what they ate.

How wrong! When seeking the good of others is truly the hallmark of Christian love.

Love is not easily angered - they needed to learn to forbear, and not drag each other off to the law-courts; it would have been better to suffer the wrong done to them than do that! Love doesn't keep a record of evil, doesn't bear grudges and it doesn't delight in evil - so no gossiping about the misdeeds of others either, and no gladness when someone else stumbles and fails. Yes, this is the Spirit's analysis of the spectrum of "agape" love, which is the Bible's special description of divine Calvary love that puts up with everything. There's nothing it can't face for it perseveres, having a tenacity buoyed up by trust and hope which enables it to pour itself out on behalf of others in every circumstance. Truly, God is love!

Lastly, in verses 8 to 13, Paul turns to the subject of the permanence of love. Love is more enduring than faith and hope. It must define how all spiritual gifts are employed in the present. The Corinthian emphasis on tongues being evidence of their false spirituality was wrong. It came from people who weren't exhibiting the one truly essential mark of the Spirit, namely Christian love. This is the love which God is by nature, which he has for the world and which his Spirit produces in us so that we show love to the Lord by keeping his commands and love to others by acts of Christian helpfulness and witness. Faith and hope by definition are not for the future - love will outlast all. It is the greatest thing because of its ability to edify others and to truly seek their good. This is the way of love. It is beyond all comparison. This is the essence and mark of Christian spirituality.

BONUS CHAPTER FIVE: ABIDING IN THE TRUE VINE

The usual biblical metaphor for our relationship with Christ is that we're members of his Church - which is biblically described as the body of which he is the head; but let's explore another metaphor in which Christ pictures himself as the vine and calls on us to abide or remain in him just like branches do in an ordinary vine. What does it mean to remain as a branch in Christ, the true Vine? Perhaps we can think in terms of our drawing spiritual sustenance directly from its supernatural source amid the daily business of our lives and our staying deeply rooted in spiritual reality. Surely, the imagery is one of "spiritual aliveness" (as opposed to spiritual dryness). We face plenty of distractions, but putting the matter of "abiding" in those terms, I feel, helps us to realize we can realistically be alive to the presence of God wherever we are.

When Christ spoke those words at the opening of John chapter 15, "I am the true vine, and My Father is the vine-dresser", he was talking in terms of the potential fruitfulness of our day-to-day relationship with himself. The point is so graphic: apart from the vine, a branch can do nothing but shrivel; and equally, if we live apart from Christ day by day, we can't be what God wants us to be as Christians. The reality of the situation is that our lives as Christians are not inevitably or automatically going to be fruitful for God. "Every branch in Me that does not bear fruit, He takes away" or "lifts up" (v.2a, NKJV margin), the Lord said.

One modern vineyard owner remarks: "New branches have a tendency to trail down and grow along the ground. We lift them up and wash them off ... they don't bear fruit down there ... get coated in dust. When it rains, they get muddy and mildewed." I suggest that could be the best way to understand what the Lord's saying here. The same word is often translated as "lifts up" in our Bibles. And so the picture becomes this: in the same way that new branches have a natural tendency to head off in less productive directions and require re-directing, so do new - and not so new – Christians sometimes need to have their energies channelled in more productive directions.

The Lord Jesus next focused his attention on branches – or believers – who were producing some fruit, when he said: "Every branch that bears fruit, He prunes it, that it may bear more fruit" (v.2b). I looked up some interesting background in a Gardening Report which told me that: "Grapevines can become so dense that the sun cannot reach into the area where fruit should form". It seems, left to itself, a grape plant will always favour new growth over more grapes. From a distance, luxurious growth is an impressive achievement, but up close, it's nothing but an underwhelming harvest.

Maybe, like me, you've been saddened to observe an experienced Christian whose life when viewed through a crisis experience seemed to display little evidence of an intimate relationship with Christ. Isn't it, sadly, our human tendency to keep up appearances, to project an impressive image, to display the leaves of our accomplishments? But the Lord comes up close, scrutinising our lives, seeking fruit. There's always the real possibility that any one of us can have seasons of abundant foliage but underneath that outward show there's little fruit. As in Eden, the leaves are a cover-up. This will only be a problem if we don't recognize what's happening and react to the action of the divine Gardener.

The Gardener's action is to cut away unnecessary shoots, because the purpose of the branch is to bear grapes. Gardeners tell us that: "because of the grape's tendency to grow so vigorously, a lot of wood must be cut away each year." So the dedicated grape-producer has, once again, to go against the plant's natural tendency. An extract from a Horticultural Bulletin runs like this: "The ability to produce growth increases each year, but without intensive pruning the plant weakens and its crop diminishes. Mature branches must be pruned hard to achieve maximum yields." There we have it - the painful reality - also for us as believers: the more mature, the more cutting! But then it's grapes, grapes and more grapes! The Lord wants us to build that kind of fruitful relationship with himself and so he uses the testing of our faith - the season of the pruning shears.

If the newer, fruitless branch needs re-directing, then the more mature, partially fruitful branch needs a reduction (of self). Living "after the Spirit", and not "after the flesh" will ensure we have more spiritual fruit and less branch visible. Still the Lord was not finished. He who came that we might have life in all its fullness, added, "He who abides in Me, and I in him, he bears much fruit." This is the point at which the Lord introduced the vital matter of our "abiding" or remaining in him as the true vine. This contains the idea of our "spiritual aliveness" - being "alive to the presence of God in our midst wherever and everywhere we are".

As David could say in the Psalms: "I have set the LORD continually before me" (Psalm 16:8). Surely abiding is all about the crucial connection which is the meeting of branch and Vine. The branch with the largest, least-obstructed connection will have greatest potential for fruit. The branch is totally dependent on the vine through that point of meeting. Fruitfulness is fundamentally about our relationship with him - if we're abiding, we will be fruitful. So far, the Lord has taught us: If the newer, fruitless branch needs re-directing and the more mature, partially fruitful branch needs reduction, then the branch aspiring to be abundantly fruitful needs to rediscover a relationship with him as the primary source of satisfaction in the Christian life. Our energies may be channelled in the right direction, our worldly ambitions may have become moderated, but is there the same dependence as in earlier days? We ought never to think we can outgrow that need for total dependence on Christ.

The Lord emphasizes the point again and again by raising the issue of 'abiding' no less than ten times here in John 15. It's on this matter of abiding that an interesting thing happens: the onus for spiritual fruitfulness in our lives now shifts from the Gardener to the branch itself - to us. It will be in the measure that we get ourselves out of the way and allow God's Word to get to work in us. Paul wrote to his Colossian friends and spoke of "the word of truth, the gospel bearing fruit and increasing in you since the day you heard it" (Colossians 1:6). When the Lord spoke of "abiding in him" he twinned that expression with "his words abiding in us" (John 15:7).

It hardly seems possible that we can experience the one without the other. Earlier in John's gospel, the Lord Jesus gives us a clear description of what it's like when people fail to allow his words to abide in them. He said to the Jews: "And the Father Himself, who sent Me, has testified of Me. You have neither heard His voice at any time, nor seen His form. But you do not have His word abiding in you, because whom He sent, Him you do not believe. You search the Scriptures, for in them you think you have eternal life; and these are they which testify of Me" (John 5:37-39).

In complete contrast, the Lord opened up to the disciples whom he met on the road to Emmaus, the things concerning Himself in all the Scriptures. The Holy Spirit will do that, as we come daily to our Bibles in our quiet times. He takes of the things of Christ there and declares them to us (John 16:14). When we experience communion like that regularly, when the Spirit of God enables us to really believe the Bible's testimony about Christ, it's then that we hear God's voice behind the sacred page – even as the Bible says, "today if you hear His voice" - and it's then we experience the reality of God's Word is abiding in us.

Branch-like intimacy and dependence develops through Bible reading and prayer that changes our desires so that they become His desires (vv.7 & 10). Then, the longings that we express in prayer align with God's will, leading us to expect to see answers to our prayers (v.7). When the praying is in relation to the Lord's work we're engaged in, this links up with aspects of fruitfulness for God in our lives (v.5) and so our heavenly Father is glorified (v.8).

This subject of abiding in Christ really starts in chapter 14 when the Lord said: "If you love Me, you will keep My commandments if anyone loves Me, he will keep My word; and My Father will love him, and We will come to him, and make Our abode with him" (see John 14:15-23). And the apostle John reserves his last recorded word on the topic of abiding for his second letter later in our Bibles: "Anyone who goes too far and does not abide in the teaching of Christ, does not have God; the one who abides in the teaching, he has both the Father and the Son". And in case there should be any doubt that the teaching of Christ - the commandments he had left for his disciples to keep - was what became known as the apostles' teaching, the very thing that defined the New Testament churches of God, John also said: "Watch yourselves, that you might not lose what we [the apostles] have accomplished, but that you may receive a full reward" (1 John 1:8-9 NASB).

Any reward in a future day when we stand before Christ will be adversely affected if there has been a lack of enthusiasm on our part to devote ourselves to the Apostolic Faith as the first believers did in Acts chapter 2. But the supreme motivation for that kind of devotion is our desire to be found abiding in Christ and being alive to his presence every moment of every day of our lives.

FURTHER TITLES IN THIS SERIES

If you've enjoyed reading this book, first of all please consider taking a moment to leave a positive review on Amazon!

Secondly, you may be interested to know that, at the date of the publishing of this book, the Search For Truth library now stands at almost fifty titles; each contains excellent reading material in a down-to-earth and conversational style, covering a wide range of topics from Bible character studies, theme studies, book studies, apologetics, prophecy, Christian living and more. The simplest way to access this material for purchase is by visiting Brian's Amazon author page:

- Amazon.com: http://amzn.to/1u7rzIA
- Amazon.co.uk: http://amzn.to/YZt5zC

Alternatively, the books can also be found simply by searching for the specific title or "Search For Truth Series" on Amazon. Paperback versions can also be purchased from Hayes Press at www.hayespress.org.

A flavour of some of the books in the library are below:

Healthy Churches: God's Bible Blueprint For Growth (FREE)

Amazon.com: http://amzn.to/1FuoN5l

Amazon.co.uk: http://amzn.to/1HTSize

As Brian notes in the opening chapters of this **FREE** book, many churches in the Western world seem to be declining in numbers and spiritual vitality. He explores some of the root causes and also how this trend could be reversed. The good news, as Brian reminds us, is that God gives us the growth blueprint in His Word through a number of key Bible words, such as sowing, reaping, planting, watering, cultivating, building and edifying. Find out the importance of each step in the process and get inspired to go for growth with, in and through, God!

PAPERBACK EDITIONS

The Supremacy of Christ

Nothing But Christ Crucified: First Corinthians

Pure Milk: Nurturing the New Life in Jesus

Once Saved, Always Saved?

Jesus: What Does The Bible Really Say?

The Tabernacle: God's House of Shadows

A Legacy of Kings: Israel's Chequered History

Healthy Churches: God's Bible Blueprint For Growth

Hope For Humanity: God's Fix For A Broken World

Fencepost Turtles: People Placed By God

Minor Prophets – Major Issues

Tribes and Tribulations – Israel's Predicted Personalities

One People For God Omnibus

Kings, Tribes and Prophets Omnibus

God – His Glory, His Building, His Son Omnibus

All these titles are also available in Kindle e-book format from Amazon.

EBOOK EDITIONS

Search For Truth Series

Apologetics

Overcoming Objections To Christian Faith

Windows To Faith

Turning The World Upside Down

An Unchanging God?

Life, the Universe and Ultimate Answers

Books of the Bible

Double Vision – The Insights Of Isaiah

Unlocking Hebrews

James – The Epistle Of Straw

The Visions of Zechariah

Experiencing God in Ephesians

Bible Character Studies

Abraham – Friend Of God

About The Bush – The Life of Moses

After God's Own Heart: The Life of David

Samson: A Type of Christ

Esther: A Date With Destiny

Discipleship

Praying With Paul

The Way: New Testament Discipleship

Power Outage: Christianity Unplugged

Closer Than A Brother – Christian Friendship

No Compromise!

Jesus Christ

Five Women And A Baby: The Genealogy of Jesus

They Met At The Cross – Five Encounters With Jesus

Salt & The Sacrifice of Christ

The Last Words of Jesus

Jesus: Son Over God's House

The Supremacy of Christ

General Topics

The Kingdom of God – Past, Present or Future?

God's Appointment Calendar: The Feasts of Jehovah

Seeds – A Potted Bible History

AWOL! Bible Deserters and Defectors

5 Sacred Solos – The Truths That The Reformation Recovered

Trees of the Bible

Knowing God: Reflections on Psalm 23

The Glory of God

Living in God's House

Answers To Listeners' Questions

Edge Of Eternity – Approaching The End Of Life

Tomorrow's Headlines – Bible Prophecy

SEARCH FOR TRUTH RADIO BROADCASTS

Search for Truth Radio has been a ministry of the Churches of God (see www.churchesofgod.info) since 1978. Free Search for Truth podcasts can be listened to online or downloaded at four locations:

- At SFT's own dedicated podcast site: www.searchfortruth.podbean.com

- Via Itunes using the podcast app (search for Search For Truth)
- On the Churches of God website: (http://www.churchesofgod.info/search_for_truth_radio_programmes.php)
- On the Transworld Radio website: (http://www.twr360.org/programs/ministry_id,103)

Alternatively, see below for details of digital and analogue radio timings.

Europe

Listen online at www.twr.org.uk/live.htm

SKY Digital Channel 0138 (11.390 GHz, ID 53555) and Freesat channel 790 and Freeview 733 in the **UK** - Saturday at 07.30 and Sunday at 06.45.

Malawi

Sunday on TWR Malawi FM Network at 06.45 UTC+2 (89.1 - 106.5 FM)

South East Asia

On Reach Beyond – Australia on Mondays 13.15 UTC, 25m band SW (15540 kHz.)

India

Tuesday and Friday on TWR Guam at 15.15, 19m band SW (15110 kHz.)

Thailand

Wednesday on TWR Guam at 08.50, 19m band SW (11965 kHz.)

Jamaica

Sunday on MegaJamz at 09.00, 98.7 FM

CONTACTING SEARCH FOR TRUTH

If you have enjoyed reading one of our books or listening to a radio broadcast, we would love to know about that, or answer any questions that you might have.

Contact us at:

SFT c/o Hayes Press, The Barn, Flaxlands, Wootton Bassett, Swindon, Wiltshire, UK SN4 8DY

P.O. Box 748, Ringwood, Victoria 3134, Australia

P.O. Box 70115, Chilomoni, Blantyre, Malawi

Web site: www.searchfortruth.org.uk

Email: sft@churchesofgod.info

Also, if you have enjoyed reading this book and/or others in the series, we would really appreciate it if you could just take a couple of minutes to leave a brief review on Amazon – it really is a very good way of spreading the word about our ministry – thanks and God bless!

Did you love *Christianity 101: Seven Basic Bible Truths*? Then you should read *First Corinthians: Nothing But Christ Crucified* by Brian Johnston!

Bible teacher Brian Johnston unpacks the first letter of the apostle Paul to the Corinthians in this informative book, exploring such important topics as spiritual gifts, the body of Christ, headcoverings, the Breaking of Bread and the powerful wisdom of God in Christ crucified!

About the Author

Born and educated in Scotland, Brian worked as a government scientist until God called him into full-time Christian ministry on behalf of the Churches of God (www.churchesofgod.info). His voice has been heard on Search For Truth radio broadcasts for over 30 years during which time he has been an itinerant Bible teacher throughout the UK and Canada. His evangelical and missionary work outside the UK is primarily in Belgium and The Philippines. He is married to Rosemary, with a son and daughter.

About the Publisher

Hayes Press (www.hayespress.org) is a registered charity in the United Kingdom, whose primary mission is to disseminate the Word of God, mainly through literature. It is one of the largest distributors of gospel tracts and leaflets in the United Kingdom, with over 100 titles and hundreds of thousands despatched annually.

Hayes Press also publishes Plus Eagles Wings, a fun and educational Bible magazine for children, six times a year and Golden Bells, a popular daily Bible reading calendar in wall or desk formats.

Also available are over 100 Bibles in many different versions, shapes and sizes, Christmas cards, Christian jewellery, Eikos Bible Art, Bible text posters and much more!

www.ingramcontent.com/pod-product-compliance
Lightning Source LLC
Chambersburg PA
CBHW071320040426
42444CB00009B/2056